GW01158245

A DAILY MAIL AND
BRITISH PATHE PRODUCTION

1947   1957   1967

THE GOLDEN YEARS

1947   *1997*

A CELEBRATION OF FIFTY GLORIOUS YEARS
OF MARRIAGE BETWEEN
Her Majesty the Queen
& Prince Philip, Duke of Edinburgh

by
PAUL JAMES

1977   *1987*   *1997*

The Golden Years

1947   1957   1967

*Travel the decades and watch the remarkable story of the Royal marriage unfold.
Follow the Royal timeline through the book as a guide to major events*

1977 *1987* *1997*

The Golden Years

First Published: August 4th 1997

All rights reserved. No part of this publication may be produced, stored in a retrieval system or transmitted in any form or by any means, electrically mechanical, photocopying, recording or otherwise, without prior permission in writing to the publisher.

British Library Cataloguing in Publication Data.

Published in Great Britain for the Daily Mail & British Pathe by Solo Books Ltd., 49-53 Kensington High Street, London W8 5ED.

ISBN No. 1 873939 11 6

© Solo Books Ltd 1997

The Beginning of a Golden Age

1977 *1987* *1997*

The Golden Years

'I, Elizabeth Alexandra Mary, take thee, Philip, to be my wedded husband, to have and to hold from this day forward...'
20th November 1947

Six years on from her marriage to the Duke of Edinburgh, Queen Elizabeth II was crowned in Westminster Abbey.
2nd June 1953

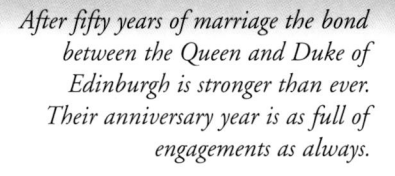

After fifty years of marriage the bond between the Queen and Duke of Edinburgh is stronger than ever. Their anniversary year is as full of engagements as always.

1947   *1957*   *1967*

Contents:

INTRODUCTION **8**

20 THE BEGINNING OF A GOLDEN AGE

THE ROYAL PROGRESS **44**

60 THE SILVER YEARS

DAWN OF A DYNASTY **80**

108 OVERRIDING THE STORMS

A GOLDEN MILESTONE **148**

1977   *1987*   *1997*

1947   1957   1967

Introduction

1977   1987   1997

The Golden Years

1947: Introduction

'I, Elizabeth Alexandra Mary, take thee, Philip, to my wedded husband, to have and to hold from this day forward...'

As the marriage vows were made and the newly created Duke of Edinburgh slipped a simple narrow band of 22-carat Welsh gold on to his young bride's finger, the bells of Westminster Abbey rang out to herald the beginning of what has now become one of the longest ever royal marriages in history.

For a nation still nursing battle scars after five years of hostilities, a royal wedding brought a much needed ray of sunshine into a dark world, where the austerity of food and clothes rationing remained as a grim reminder of war. 'A splash of colour on the hard road we have to travel' was how Winston Churchill described the day.

To the British people, the marriage of King George VI's eldest daughter and heir, Princess Elizabeth, to the handsome Lieutenant Philip Mountbatten, symbolised hope for the future. The first major royal occasion and cause for celebration since the victory parades of 1945, saw the country overtaken by wedding fever. In a family where marriages had so often been for political alliance in the past, this was unquestionably a love-match; a true-life fairy-tale romance that deserved a happy ending.

PREVIOUS PAGE: *Princess Elizabeth attends 'The Sleeping Beauty' The Royal Opera House, March 1946*

LEFT: *The Wedding party, November 1947*

ABOVE: *Wedding Day smiles from the balcony; the Bride and Groom, the Queen and Lady Mary Cambridge, November 1947*

1947   1957   1967

Introduction

'She won't give her heart lightly, but when she does it will be for always,' Queen Mary had confided to an old friend about her granddaughter. 'It does sometimes happen that one falls in love early, and it lasts forever. Elizabeth seems to me that kind of girl.' Her words were prophetic, for Princess Elizabeth fell in love with the first man she ever met and has never wavered in her devotion.

Since the heavy mantle of sovereignty fell upon her shoulders on the sudden death of her father, Prince Philip has been the rock and support from which she has gained her strength. In 1948 her mother had described wedded life as 'the highest form of human fellowship'. After fifty years of marriage, the Queen and Prince Philip are in full accordance with this sentiment.

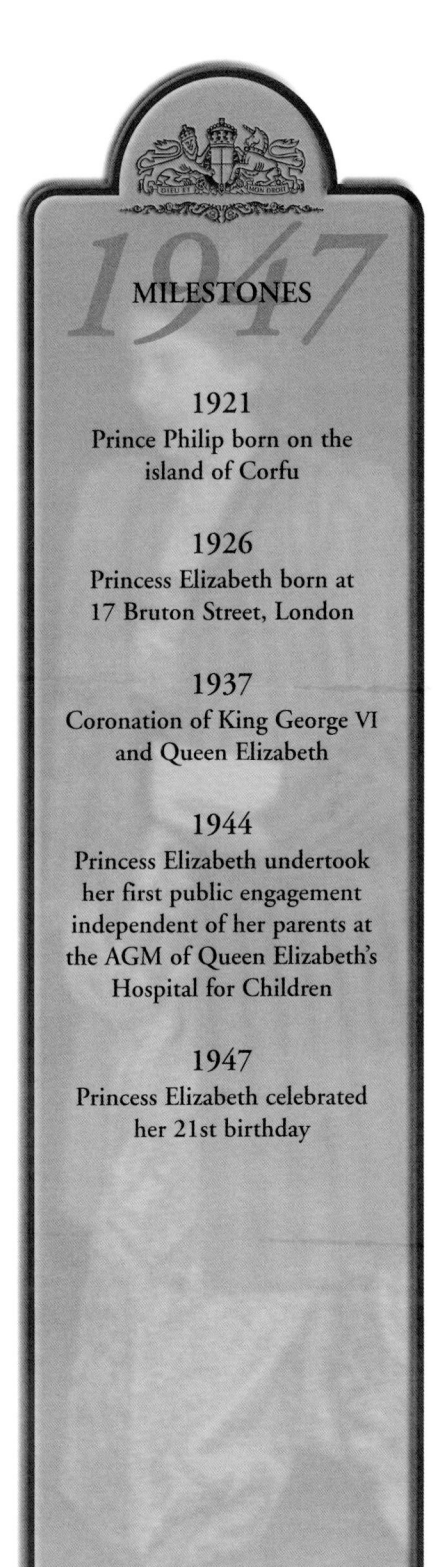

MILESTONES

1921
Prince Philip born on the island of Corfu

1926
Princess Elizabeth born at 17 Bruton Street, London

1937
Coronation of King George VI and Queen Elizabeth

1944
Princess Elizabeth undertook her first public engagement independent of her parents at the AGM of Queen Elizabeth's Hospital for Children

1947
Princess Elizabeth celebrated her 21st birthday

1977   *1987*   *1997*

The Golden Years

LEFT: *Princess Elizabeth chats with the the Dowager Countess of Airlie, August, 1931*

RIGHT: *King George V and Queen Mary with Princess Elizabeth leaving Westminster Abbey, July 1934*

Five years after Prince Philip was born, Princess Elizabeth came into the world feet first by Caesarean section at 2.43am on 21 April, 1926. Born at 17 Bruton Street, London W1, the home of her maternal grandparents, Elizabeth was later to enter the history books as the first monarch to have been born in a private house. As the first born child of the then Duke and Duchess of York (later King George VI and Queen Elizabeth) it seemed unlikely that she would ever accede to the throne. She might eventually have a brother who would take precedence. Her uncle the Prince of Wales was heir-apparent, free to marry and produce heirs of his own. No-one could possibly forsee the path that lay ahead.

The popular story of the gallant yet penniless Greek who won the heart of a King's daughter captured the public's imagination, but is not altogether founded on fact. Prince Philip was born on the island of Corfu on 10 June 1921, but his ancestry is not Greek. His father, Prince Andrew, was of the Royal House of Denmark; his mother, Princess Alice (Lord Louis Mountbatten's sister) was English and a great-granddaughter of Queen Victoria. Philip's boyhood home was in England, he was educated at Cheam School in Berkshire and Gordonstoun in Scotland, and entered the British Royal Navy as a career. Although Princess Elizabeth was third in line to the throne at the time of her birth, Prince Philip was also sixth in line to the throne of Greece and the couple are in fact third cousins through their descent from Queen Victoria. Thus, the gulf that appears to exist in their backgrounds is less deep than generally believed.

1947   *1957*   *1967*

Introduction

The British public took an extraordinary interest in Princess Elizabeth from the moment of her birth. Crowds gathered daily outside her parent's home at 145 Piccadilly. It was reported that open-topped buses, which still plied London's streets, were seen to lean sideways as they passed the house, with passengers rushing across to peer into the nursery window.

By the age of three Princess Elizabeth was known as 'the Empire's Darling' and appeared on the cover of the American magazine *Time*. When it was revealed that her nursery clothes were yellow, a new fashion was instantly created. Pinks and blues were out for toddlers. For Christmas the Princess was given her first pony and long queues formed outside Madame Tussaud's when a waxwork of the Princess astride a Shetland pony was put on display. Soon her young face appeared on chocolate boxes, china mugs and plates, and her first ever postage stamp. When her sister Princess Margaret Rose was born in 1930, interest in the 'little Princesses' became insatiable.

1977   *1987*   *1997*

13

The Golden Years

In contrast, the young Prince Philip spent a less public childhood living quietly at Broadlands, the Mountbatten home in Hampshire, and travelling widely between relatives in Europe, unaware that the full glare of the spotlight would one day fall on him too.

Although Prince Philip was on the periphery of the royal circle and visited Buckingham Palace with his mother for tea with Queen Mary, there was no early contact with his future wife. For a woman who has now travelled the globe, Princess Elizabeth had a very sheltered upbringing. She was educated privately, had few friends and Princess Margaret was her closest companion. For them, a trip to Eastbourne with afternoon tea in an hotel was considered an adventure. Doing 'ordinary' things, such as riding in an underground train or bus were major expeditions. Swimming lessons at the Bath Club were high spots of the week and a rare occasion when they mixed with other children. Ironically, Prince Philip had a much fuller and more eventful life.

ABOVE: *Princess Elizabeth at the Aldershot Tattoo, June 1938*

RIGHT: *Princess Elizabeth leaving the Bath Club where she used to go for swimming lessons, May 1938.*

1947   *1957*   *1967*

In November 1934 Philip's cousin Princess Marina married Elizabeth's uncle, the Duke of Kent. Although both youngsters were present at the wedding, neither remember each other. Almost five more years were to pass before they met again. On 22nd July 1939 the King and Queen paid an official weekend visit to the Royal Naval College at Dartmouth where Prince Philip was a cadet. Having just won swimming prizes at the Bath Club, Princesses Elizabeth and Margaret were allowed to join their parents as a reward. Due to bad weather, the Princesses were entertained at the Captain's house with a model railway. 'A fairhaired boy, rather like a Viking, with a sharp face and piercing blue eyes entered the room,' wrote their governess Marion Crawford. He knelt beside Princess Elizabeth at the railway; later they played croquet when the sun came out, and sat near each other at lunch. In the afternoon Prince Philip escorted the young Princesses around the College grounds and, it is said, showed-off by jumping over the tennis nets.

The following day Princess Elizabeth entertained him to tea, watching wide-eyed as Philip devoured a large plateful of shrimps. When the Royal Yacht finally departed, Prince Philip followed in a small rowing boat until forced to turn back. Princess Elizabeth watched through her binoculars until he was just a speck on the horizon.

1977   *1987*   *1997*

The Golden Years

Within weeks they met again at a private family party at Royal Lodge but, because of the age gap, the 13-year-old Princess was more smitten than the 18-year-old cadet. With the outbreak of war on 3rd September 1939 Philip was posted as midshipman to the convoy battleship *HMS Ramillies,* while the Princess was incarcerated with her sister at Windsor Castle. Elizabeth began writing to Philip, sending him food parcels and knitted socks.

As early as January 1941 there were rumours that Elizabeth and Philip would marry. She was blossoming into womanhood; he was maturing fast. Involved in the Battle of Cape Matapan, Philip described the experience as 'near murder as anything could be in wartime.' On leave that October, Philip had tea with the Royal Family and entertained the gathering with stories of his daring exploits. Queen Mary believed that it was the moment Elizabeth fell in love. A month later Elizabeth and Philip danced together for the first time at a family party.

LEFT: *The two princesses arrive back at Waterloo, May 1939*

TOP RIGHT: *Princess Elizabeth on her way to the launching of the new carrier HMS Bugle at Belfast, March 1946*

BOTTOM RIGHT: *The Sword of State borne by the Lord Major preceded the Royal Family at St. Paul's Thanksgiving service for Tunisia, May 1943*

1947   1957   1967

Duty kept Philip away from England for much of the war, but each time he was on leave the King and Queen invited him to visit them. He and the Princess took long walks together, talking animatedly. Philip wanted a permanent career in the British Navy, but was still officially of Greek nationality and now third in line to the Greek throne, even though he had lived in England since the age of eight.

By 1944 Princess Elizabeth knew for certain that she was falling in love with Philip although her parents dismissed it as infatuation. 'We both think she is too young for that now,' King George VI wrote to his mother Queen Mary, 'She has never met any young men of her own age.' Prince Philip was nevertheless included in the guest list for a private family lunch party to celebrate Princess Elizabeth's eighteenth birthday that year. When he returned to sea, the couple began a serious and regular correspondence that can only be described as a courtship, with letters travelling by diplomatic mail for security. It was noted that a photograph of Philip appeared on the mantlepiece in the Princess's private sitting-room. 'People might talk,' the Princess was warned. Not to be thwarted, she replaced it with a rare photograph of the Prince with a beard.

At the end of the war, Princesses Elizabeth and Margaret joined in the VE Day celebrations by mingling incognito with the crowds outside the Palace. Never before had the two mixed so freely amongst the people. 'I think it was one of the most memorable nights of my life,' said Princess Elizabeth. That night the King wrote sadly in his diary of his daughters, 'Poor darlings, they have never had any fun yet.'

1977   *1987*   *1997*

1947   1957   1967

THE 47-57 ROYAL DECADE
The Beginning of a Golden Age

1977   1987   1997

The Golden Years

1947-1957:
The Beginning of a Golden Age

Buckingham Palace
10th July, 1947

It is with the greatest pleasure that The King and Queen announce the betrothal of their dearly beloved daughter The Princess Elizabeth to Lieutenant Philip Mountbatten, RN, son of the late Prince Andrew of Greece and Princess Andrew (Princess Alice of Battenberg) to which union The King has gladly given consent.

The news of the royal engagement was received with universal joy and satisfaction. Philip Mountbatten was seen as virile, attractive and a popular choice. Thousands gathered outside Buckingham Palace in the hope of catching a glimpse of the happy pair and were not disappointed. The couple attended a service at Westminster Abbey for the unveiling of a Battle of Britain Memorial and later attended a Buckingham Palace garden party, where crowds strained to catch a glimpse of the engagement ring.

Even more well-wishers converged in The Mall that evening shouting, 'We want Elizabeth! We want Philip!' until both came out on to the balcony to loud and incessant cheers.

1947   1957   1967

22

The Beginning of a Golden Age

Philip gave the Princess a platinum engagement ring set with eleven diamonds, taken from a tiara that had belonged to his mother. Princess Alice, now a nun, was able to have the ring made at the London firm of Philip Antrobus Ltd without anyone suspecting who it was for. With the remaining stones, Philip designed a diamond bracelet which he gave to his bride on their wedding day.

PREVIOUS PAGE: *The Princess and Duke making a short walk from Her Majesty's Theatre to their awaiting car, May 1951*

BELOW: *Princess Elizabeth and Lieutenant Mountbatten are joined on the balcony of Buckingham Palace by the King and Queen and Princess Margaret, July 1947*

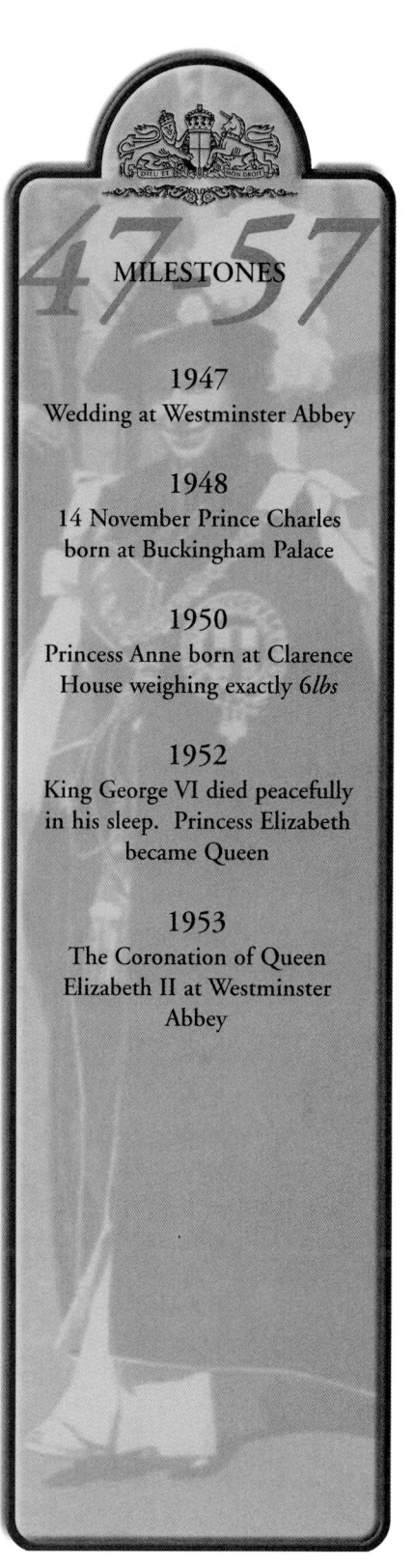

MILESTONES

1947
Wedding at Westminster Abbey

1948
14 November Prince Charles born at Buckingham Palace

1950
Princess Anne born at Clarence House weighing exactly 6*lbs*

1952
King George VI died peacefully in his sleep. Princess Elizabeth became Queen

1953
The Coronation of Queen Elizabeth II at Westminster Abbey

1977   *1987*   *1997*

The Golden Years

As a foretaste of the future, Philip immediately began accompanying the Princess on official duties. Barely were the engagement celebrations over than they were on their way to Scotland, where the Princess received the Freedom of Edinburgh at the Usher Hall on 16th July. As Heiress Presumptive, Elizabeth began to take a more active official role and accompanied her father at the State Opening of Parliament for the first time. Philip continued in his appointment on the staff of the R.N. Petty Officers' Training School at Corsham. He took an active part in their work and play, and had the reputation of being a good all-round cricketer.

LEFT: *The Princess arrives at a hotel for dinner before going on to open a dance in Edinburgh, July 1947*

RIGHT: *Princess Elizabeth drove with the King and Queen from Buckingham Palace to open the third session of Parliament, October 1947*

1947   *1957*   *1967*

The Beginning of a Golden Age

On the eve of the wedding, as crowds were already taking up their places along the processional route, King George VI granted Philip royal status and on the wedding day itself - 20th November 1947 created him Baron Greenwich, Earl of Merioneth and Duke of Edinburgh. It was seen as the final touch to the romantic picture.

With clothes rationing still in force Princess Elizabeth was subject to a clothing allowance like any other bride and was granted the standard allotment of extra coupons. Queen Mary had additional material locked away in readiness and endless parcels of silk and lace arrived from around the world.

The ivory satin wedding dress was designed by Norman Hartnell, on which white roses of York had been hand embroidered in ten thousand pearls and crystals. The veil was held in place by a diamond fringe tiara made in 1830, which Elizabeth had borrowed from her mother. Twenty-six years later she loaned it to her own daughter, Princess Anne.

Presents poured in from loyal subjects including 32,000 food parcels which were distributed to needy widows and pensioners. Princess Margaret gave her sister a picnic set; Lord Louis Mountbatten donated a cinema screen and projector. From countless pairs of nylon stockings to a strip of cloth hand-spun by Mahatma Gandhi, over 1,500 gifts were put on display at St. James's Palace.

1977 *1987* *1997*

The Golden Years

When Princess Elizabeth decided to wear two strands of historic pearls that had been a gift from her parents, she discovered that they were amongst the display. Her Private Secretary, John Colville, had to dash to St. James's Palace to fetch them and faced difficulty convincing the police that he had royal permission to collect the pearls and that he was not just a very audacious thief!

Princess Elizabeth travelled to Westminster Abbey with the King in the Irish State Coach. Eight bridesmaids, including Princess Margaret, and two page boys followed her down the aisle. With the Abbey filled to capacity and half the world glued to their wireless sets, the couple were married by the then Archbishop of Canterbury, Geoffrey Fisher, in a traditional ceremony. It was noted that the Princess promised to 'obey' her husband. With few television sets in the country, the general public later flocked to the cinemas to see the new Duke and Duchess of Edinburgh courtesy of Pathe newsreels.

1947   *1957*   *1967*

The Beginning of a Golden Age

TOP LEFT: *The couple wave from the balcony at Buckingham Palace, November 1947*

BOTTOM LEFT: *Front page of The Daily Mail, November 21, 1947*

TOP RIGHT: *The Royal Wedding cake*

BOTTOM RIGHT: *The Wedding party at the Palace after the ceremony*

The newly married couple rode back in the Glass Coach through the streets thronging with cheering well wishers. Later they appeared on the balcony of Buckingham Palace to deafening cheers. At the wedding breakfast, a nine-feet high, four-tiered wedding cake awaited them, which they cut with a ceremonial sword. For a country where sugar was still rationed, the cake received almost as much admiration as the bride's dress.

'Notwithstanding the splendour and national significance of the service in this Abbey,' said the Archbishop of York in an address to the bride and groom, 'it is in all essentials the same as it would be for any cottager who might be married this afternoon in some small country church in a remote village in the dales. The same vows are taken; the same prayers are offered; and the same blessings are given.'

1977   1987   1997

The Golden Years

Chased by bridesmaids and showered with rose petals, the couple later left Buckingham Palace in an open landau bound for Waterloo station. He in his naval uniform, she in 'love-in-the-mist' blue. They honeymooned at Broadlands, the Mountbatten home in Hampshire and at Birkhall on the Balmoral estate.

Before departing for Scotland, Elizabeth and Philip issued a personal message to the general public: 'We want to say the reception given to us on our wedding day and the loving interest shown by our fellow countrymen and well-wishers in all parts of the world, have left an impression which will never grow faint. We can find no words to express what we feel, but we can at least offer our grateful thanks to the millions who have given us this unforgettable send-off in our married life.'

1947   *1957*   *1967*

The Beginning of a Golden Age

The first marital home was at Windlesham Moor in Berkshire, where Princess Elizabeth came the closest she would ever come to being a housewife. Although the Duke of Edinburgh continued with his naval duties, he became a working member of the Royal Family.

On 14th May 1948 Elizabeth and Philip paid a State visit to Paris, where the Princess opened an exhibition depicting British life. They visited Versailles and Fontainbleau, attended receptions, watched racing at Longchamp and saw a ballet at the Paris Opera House. Although she could speak fluent French, it was the Princess's first visit to the Continent and Prince Philip proved to be an invaluable escort. As a seasoned traveller, and having spent some of his childhood in Paris, he felt completely at ease and it proved a good induction for the many overseas visits that lay ahead.

On returning from France, Princess Elizabeth began restricting her public engagements as she was expecting their first child. Less than a year after their wedding, crowds were gathering once again around the gates of Buckingham Palace for news of the impending birth, Prince Charles was born at 9.14pm on Sunday 14th November 1948. The fountains in Trafalgar Square were floodlit blue for a week to celebrate the birth of a boy and the nation rejoiced at the news.

FAR LEFT: *Rose petals shower the newly married Royal couple, November 1947*

LEFT: *Princess Elizabeth and the Duke of Edinburgh in the Royal Box at the Opera House, Paris, May 1948*

ABOVE: *Princess Elizabeth opening the exhibition at Musée Gallicia in France, May 1948*

1977　　　　　　　　　*1987*　　　　　　　　　*1997*

The Golden Years

Just when Elizabeth and Philip's happiness should have been complete, the King's health began to deteriorate through defective blood circulation in his legs. A planned tour to Australia and New Zealand was postponed. The Duke of Edinburgh cancelled his return to the Navy, as he and the Princess represented the King in the months that followed.

In March 1949 the King underwent a lung operation and as Heir Presumptive, Princess Elizabeth accepted Clarence House near Buckingham Palace as an official home. After extensive refurbishment to the house, the Edinburghs moved in on 4th July. That year, for the first time, Princess Elizabeth deputised for her father at Trooping the Colour.

LEFT: *Princess Elizabeth names Belfast's first flying boat 'Aotearoa II' built by Short Bros in Harland, May 1949*

RIGHT: *Princess Elizabeth and Prince Charles on the train bound for Balmoral, September 1950*

1947   1957   1967

The Beginning of a Golden Age

When the King's health appeared to improve, Philip resumed his naval career and returned to the Mediterranean as First Lieutenant on the destroyer *HMS Chequers*. Not wishing to be separated for long, Princess Elizabeth flew out to Malta to join him for two months, from March to May 1950. It was the first and only time that she was to experience being a normal wife without any official duties.

In July 1950, the Duke of Edinburgh was promoted to the rank of Lieutenant-Commander and took command of the frigate *HMS Magpie*. Before taking up his duties, the Duke flew home to England for the birth of their second child. On 15th August 1950 five years to the day since the surrender of Japan, where Prince Philip was serving in the Pacific - Princess Elizabeth gave birth to a girl.

The baby, weighing exactly 6lb, was the only one of the future Queen's children to be born at Clarence House. The Test Match at the Oval was interrupted briefly to announce the new arrival. Half-an-hour after she was born, the baby Princess was elected as the millionth member of the Automobile Association, as membership reached one million on that very day. The birth was registered two weeks later and she was given the names Anne Elizabeth Alice Louise. At the same time the baby was given a yellow identity card, a green ration book and an entitlement to orange juice and cod liver oil.

The Golden Years

Shortly after the birth of Princess Anne, the Duke of Edinburgh returned to the Mediterranean to take up his command of *HMS Magpie*. This proved to be the final stage of his active career as princely duties would soon make demands on his life.

On 3 May 1951 King George VI opened the Festival of Britain, looking pale and drawn. A short time later he had an attack of influenza from which recovery appeared slow. A leading chest surgeon was called in, who confirmed the Royal Family's worst fears: the King had cancer.

The removal of one lung was essential if the King were to live, yet the very life-saving operation itself could possibly cause a coronary attack. It was also necessary to remove some of the nerves in the King's larynx, which meant that the man who had suffered a severe stutter most of his life might only ever speak in a faint whisper.

RIGHT: *The Princess arriving at a reception in her honour at the City Chambers Glasgow, May 1951*

The Beginning of a Golden Age

ABOVE: *Princess Elizabeth waving goodbye to the people of St. John New Brunswick, November 9, 1951*

RIGHT: *Princess Elizabeth and the Duke of Edinburgh leaving London Airport in the BOAC Stratocruiser Canopus for their Canadian tour, October 1951*

A lung resection operation proved successful and by October 1951 it was deemed safe for Princess Elizabeth and the Duke of Edinburgh to embark on a tour of Canada and the United States. An enthusiastic welcome was given throughout the five weeks of official engagements. President Truman declared that Elizabeth was the fairy Princess of his childhood books come to life. During the tour the Royal couple travelled long distances by train, offering a rare chance for them to be alone. On one occasion staff were amazed to see the Prince wearing a large set of joke false teeth, chasing the Princess along the corridor. It became their private joke, and before a public appearance Prince Philip would whisper in his wife's ear, 'Remember the wailing and gnashing of teeth!'

The Golden Years

At the end of January 1952 Princess Elizabeth and the Duke of Edinburgh set off on another Royal tour of East Africa, Australia and New Zealand. Following a thorough medical examination, King George VI was taken to London Airport to wave them off as they boarded the BOAC Argonaut airliner *Atlanta* that was to take them to Kenya on the first stage of the tour. Looking frail, the King stood in the bitter cold to wave goodbye. It was to be a final farewell.

At some time during the night of Wednesday 6 February King George VI died peacefully in his sleep. Far away in Nairobi Princess Elizabeth was watching wild life in the African bush, unaware that she was now Queen, almost certainly sitting in a tree at the moment of accession. At 2.45pm local time, 11.45am in Britain, the Duke of Edinburgh broke the news to his young wife. News she bore with courage and calmness. The remainder of the tour was cancelled and they returned to England to bear the burden of her new responsibilities. When asked what name she would choose as Queen, she replied, 'My own name - what else ?'

1947   *1957*   *1967*

The Beginning of a Golden Age

TOP LEFT: *Sir Gerald Wollaston, Norroy and Ulster King of Arms reads the Proclamation of Queen Elizabeth II, Queen of the Realm, February 1952*

BOTTOM LEFT: *The Royal Proclamation being read for the 4th time from the steps of the Royal Exchange*

ABOVE: *The funeral procession leaves Sandringham, February 1952*

A group of Privy Councillors, headed by the Prime Minister Winston Churchill, assembled at London Airport to receive Queen Elizabeth the Second. It was a pathetic young figure, clad in black, whom they saw come down the gangway from the plane. Fragile she may have looked, but she had inner strength and accepted the high duty of sovereignty now vested in her. Prince Philip, it was noted, looked as if the weight of the world had landed on his shoulders.

The following day the Garter King at Arms, Sir George Bellew, read the first public proclamation of the accession of Queen Elizabeth from the scarlet draped balcony of Friary Court, St. James's Palace. A new Elizabethan era had begun. On 15th February the funeral of King George VI took place at St. George's Chapel, Windsor. As Elizabeth II scattered earth on her father's coffin, the whole country observed two minutes silence.

1977   *1987*   *1997*

The Golden Years

On 24th March 1953 Queen Mary died at Marlborough House aged 85, just ten weeks before the Coronation. 'What perfect timing!' said an official at the BBC wickedly, 'In between the Boat Race and the Grand National.' It had been Queen Mary's implicit instruction that if she should die, the Coronation should go ahead as planned. At the funeral, grief showed strongly in the young Queen's face; in the space of one year she had been robbed of the two greatest influences in her life. She needed Prince Philip's strength and support more than ever before.

Coronation Day, 2nd June, dawned grey and wet, and it continued to drizzle throughout the day. After a year of preparation Queen Elizabeth II was to be crowned in Westminster Abbey where she had been married nearly six years earlier. The last remaining drop of oil with which the sovereign is annointed had been destroyed during the Second World War. A new batch was made by a Bond Street chemist from the original formula that dated from the Coronation of Charles I.

1947   *1957*   *1967*

The Beginning of a Golden Age

The Queen's Coronation dress was created by Norman Hartnell. Made from white satin, it was richly embroidered with all the emblems of Great Britain and the Commonwealth. Into the Irish shamrock Hartnell had secretly embroidered a four-leaf clover for luck. The Imperial State Crown that the Queen was to wear after the ceremony and on all subsequent State Openings of Parliament was made smaller, but to get used to the heavy St. Edward's Crown, the official crown of England, weighing 2.25kg, the Queen often wore it around the Palace beforehand, even whilst feeding the corgis.

TOP LEFT: *The Queen leaves the Abbey, Coronation Day, June 1953*

TOP RIGHT: *A service of Thanksgiving and Dedication at St. Giles' Cathedral as the Duke of Hamilton on bended knee, receives the Crown of Scotland from the Queen*

LEFT: *The Queen's message on the front page of The Daily Mail, June 3, 1953*

1977   1987   1997

The Golden Years

Some 30,000 people slept in The Mall outside Buckingham Palace to await the procession. The Queen was enthroned on King Edward's Chair which contained the Coronation Stone - the Stone of Destiny - said to be the pillow on which Jacob slept. Geoffrey Fisher, Archbishop of Canterbury, raised St. Edward's Crown high above Her Majesty's head and let it slowly and majestically descend. It was precisely 12.33pm and 30 seconds. 'God Save the Queen' echoed shouts from inside the Abbey. Trumpets heralded the crowning, bells peeled, cannons fired, the people cheered, and some 700 million people around the world felt the warmth of patriotic pride.

The Queen and Prince Philip moved to Buckingham Palace, where the Prince set about making changes to ensure the day-to-day running was more efficient. Their furniture was moved from Clarence House to their own apartments, and they made a conscious decision that their family life should not be destroyed. Time was set aside every day to spend with their children so that they should not become strangers. In all matters, Philip became protective of his wife and outspoken if necessary. He was able to express views where it would have been impossible for the Queen to speak her mind, and was prepared to take criticism for it. Through fifty years of marriage his shielding of the Queen has remained unchanged.

1947   *1957*   *1967*

The Beginning of a Golden Age

LEFT: *'We want the Queen!' cried the crowds from The Mall and at 5.30pm the newly crowned Queen appeared. A young prince Charles and Princess Anne wave to the crowds, June 1953*

BELOW: *The Queen and the Duke of Edinburgh acknowledge a warm and loyal welcome at the start of their 27 hour tour of Gibraltar, May 1954*

However much they may have craved a normal family life, duty was demanding. In November 1953 they embarked on a tour of the Commonwealth that was to take them away from their children for six months, a tour which included Bermuda, Jamaica, Fiji, Tonga and New Zealand from where the Queen broadcast her Christmas message from Government House, Auckland. After two months in Australia the tour took them to Ceylon, Uganda, Libya, Malta and Gibraltar, where they were finally reunited with Prince Charles and Princess Anne. 'I don't think they knew who we were,' the Queen admitted sadly. Crowds gathered along the banks of the River Thames on 15th May, 1954, to watch their return to London.

1977　　　　　　　　　　1987　　　　　　　　　　1997

The Golden Years

Despite the tumultuous welcome home, the Queen and the Duke of Edinburgh faced a major crisis within the family. Princess Margaret had fallen in love with Group Captain Peter Townsend, the Comptroller of the Household at Clarence House. Rumours had begun after the Coronation ceremony itself, when Margaret was seen picking a thread from his uniform and brushing his jacket with an affectionate look. Later the Princess made her wish known to the Queen that she and Peter Townsend wished to marry - an impossibility under the Royal Marriages Act as he had divorced in 1952.

BELOW: *The Royal children watch their father play polo at Smith's Lawn, Windsor Great park, June 1955*

RIGHT: *The Queen listens to a speech of welcome delivered by a blind man at the Oji River Leper Settlement, Nigeria, November 1957*

FAR RIGHT: *Princess Margaret's decision hits the headlines, The Daily Mail November 1, 1955*

1947   1957   1967

The Beginning of a Golden Age

Although the innocent party, marriage between the monarch's sister and a divorced servant was out of the question. The Queen desperately wanted to avoid a scandal and asked Princess Margaret to wait until the following August when she would be twenty five, hoping perhaps that she would then feel differently. By the autumn of 1955 however, Princess Margaret's love had not cooled. Both parties were besieged by photographers as the matter came to a head. In October Parliament decided that the Princess could marry Peter Townsend, but only on the condition that she renounce her rights to the succession and relinquish her Civil List allowance. After much soul searching, Princess Margaret decided to place duty before her own personal happiness.

For the Queen and Prince Philip life was settling into a pattern. They were a popular partnership on overseas tours. On a three week visit to Nigeria in February 1956 they adopted a leper child financially, to the delight of the colony leader. 'This will do more to conquer man's fear and hate of the disease,' he said, 'than any other single act I can think of.'

At home they introduced informal lunches at the Palace to enable them to meet people from all walks of life. Thus, the Queen was able to entertain the Soviet leader Nikita Khruschev one day and lunch with actors and businessmen the next. In contrast, with a growing political crisis over Suez, the Queen signed a proclamation calling up army reserves in case of war.

1977   1987   1997

The Golden Years

In their personal life, duty separated them once again. 'It soon became obvious that there were a good many island communities and outposts in the Indian Ocean, the South Pacific, Antarctic and Atlantic which cannot be visited by air and which are too remote and too small to get into the more usual tours', revealed the Duke. Thus a three-month long tour was planned, during which he was able to open the Olympic Games in Melbourne. Unfortunately it meant being away from the Queen on their wedding anniversary and over Christmas. 'Of all the voices we have heard this afternoon,' said the Queen in her Christmas Day broadcast that year, 'none has given my children and myself greater joy than that of my husband.'

LEFT: *The Duke of Edinburgh wearing uniform of the 4/5 Battalion Queen's Cameron Highlanders, August 1955*

ABOVE: *The Queen presents a silver cup to Brigadier Masood Ali Beg, winner of the polo match in Windsor Park, May 1956*

1947　　　　　　　　　1957　　　　　　　　　1967

The Beginning of a Golden Age

Three-hundred journalists and two-hundred photographers awaited their eventual re-union in February 1957, which took place on a State Visit by the Queen to Portugal. The tour gained something of a carnival atmosphere and the couple were showered with rose petals and confetti.

As their first decade of marriage came to a close, the Queen rewarded the Duke with a new title for his services to the Commonwealth. Although he had been popularly known as 'Prince Philip' throughout their marriage, due to an oversight by King George VI, Philip was officially only a Baron, an Earl and a Duke. The Queen put the matter right in 1957 and her consort husband was granted 'the style and dignity of a Prince of the United Kingdom'. It was a fitting gift from the monarch to her husband.

ABOVE: *Prince Philip offers a lift to Mr Adams the Vingtenier of Sark while riding in an open top Victoria, July 1957*

1947   *1957*   *1967*

THE
The Royal Progress
57-67
ROYAL DECADE

1977   1987   1997

The Golden Years

1957-1967:
The Royal Progress

By the late 1950's Prince Philip was anxious that the Royal Family should be seen to move with the times and make themselves more accessible. Breaking with tradition, Prince Charles was enrolled at Hill House School, and later went on to Cheam where his father had been educated, thus becoming the first heir apparent to go to school rather than receive private tutelage, 'The Queen and I want Charles to go to school with other boys of his generation,' said the Duke, 'and learn to live with other children, and to absorb from childhood the discipline imposed by education with others.'

PREVIOUS PAGE: *The Queen and Prince Philip's visit to Freetown on the tour of Sierra Leone, November 1961*

Realising the impact made by televising the Coronation, Prince Philip began to explore this broadcasting medium as a way of bringing the Monarchy closer to the people. Television cameras already followed them everywhere and now he tested the waters by making a film about his travels in Antarctica.

At the end of 1957, the Queen's Christmas Day broadcast was televised for the first time. 'It is inevitable that I should seem a rather remote figure to many of you - a successor to the Kings and Queens of history,' she began, 'but now at least for a few minutes I welcome you to the peace of my own home.' At the close of the broadcast, thinking that the cameras had been turned off, she gave her husband a beaming smile of relief. It was a natural human reaction that brought her much praise. 'In all its long history,' Harold Macmillan told her, 'the Crown has never stood so high.'

LEFT: *The artist Devas working on a new picture of the Queen, April 1958*

RIGHT: *After landing at London Airport, Prince Philip met up with the Queen and Prince Charles to attend a reception committee of Cabinet Ministers and BOAC officials, May 1959*

1947   *1957*   *1967*

The Royal Progress

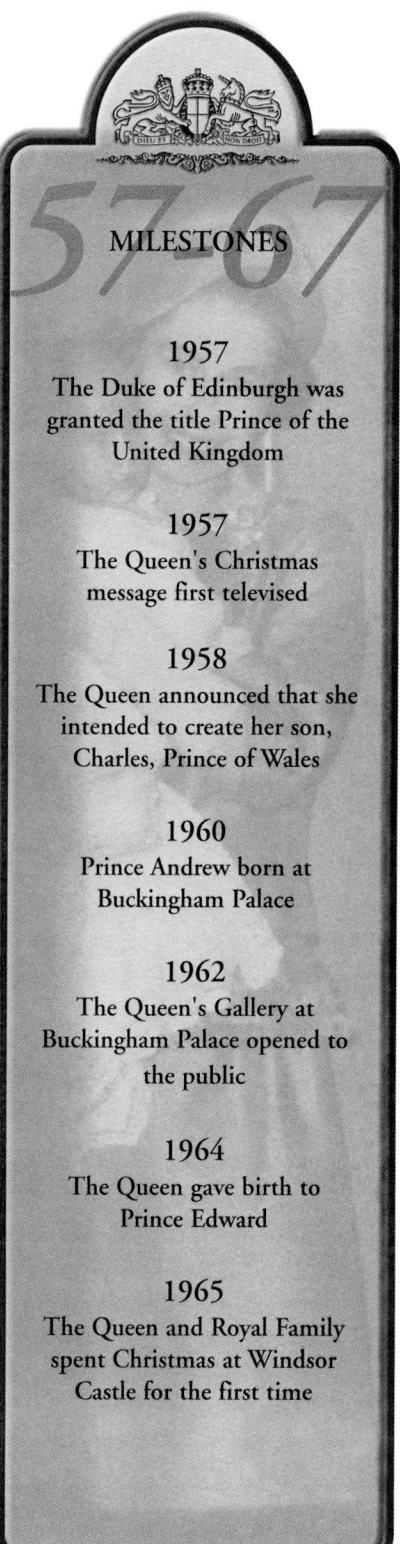

MILESTONES

1957
The Duke of Edinburgh was granted the title Prince of the United Kingdom

1957
The Queen's Christmas message first televised

1958
The Queen announced that she intended to create her son, Charles, Prince of Wales

1960
Prince Andrew born at Buckingham Palace

1962
The Queen's Gallery at Buckingham Palace opened to the public

1964
The Queen gave birth to Prince Edward

1965
The Queen and Royal Family spent Christmas at Windsor Castle for the first time

1977   1987   1997

The Golden Years

The State Opening of Parliament was televised for the first time in 1958 and, as a further move forward, the Queen discontinued the annual presentation of debutantes at court. The number of Buckingham Palace garden parties were increased, which enabled her to meet a wider range of people from vastly different backgrounds. On 26th July 1958 a popular announcement was made that the Queen intended to create her eldest son Prince of Wales. The historic tape-recorded message was played at the closing ceremony of the British and Commonwealth Games in Cardiff.

The royal year continued to be mapped out well in advance, with unavoidable perennial engagements - the Maundy Service, Trooping the Colour, the Order of the Garter ceremony, Remembrance Sunday - pencilled in first, and the day-to-day diary filled in around them. Weekly visits the length and breadth of the British Isles, opening buildings, visiting schools, hospitals, charities, factories, attending dinners and gala functions, were the visible side of their public life. Behind the scenes were endless meetings with politicians and advisers, portrait sittings, audiences, investitures and garden parties, state banquets and informal luncheons. At least twice a year there were lengthy overseas tours to the Queen's other realms and territories.

LEFT: *The Queen is presented with a blue blanket by 3 year old Charles Early at Witney near Oxford, April 1959*

RIGHT: *The Queen and the Duke at Trooping the Colour*

1947   *1957*   *1967*

The Royal Progress

Throughout March and April 1959 Prince Philip toured India, Pakistan, Hong Kong, Singapore, Sarawak, Bahamas, North Borneo and the Solomon Islands. In 100 days he circled the globe. He returned to England in May for a hectic round of engagements with the Queen. At the Chelsea Flower Show he examined a new automatic sprinkler system for gardens and soaked the surrounding press photographers. From the Duke's jaunty mood, no-one could be certain that it was accidental.

1977   *1987*   *1997*

The Golden Years

Three weeks later on 18th June 1959 the Queen and Prince Philip flew to Canada for the dedication of the newly opened St. Lawrence Seaway. The 45 day tour involved a full schedule in sweltering heat, visiting dusty mines, travelling long distances over bumpy roads, and they were greeted by enthusiastic crowds, even though a new national anthem, *O Canada*, replaced *God Save The Queen*. Only the concerned Duke of Edinburgh knew that his wife was expecting their third child. The Queen refused to cancel any of the gruelling itinerary, but the press quickly noticed how exhausted she appeared. Eventually she was forced to take a couple of day's rest. Instead of returning by sea as planned at the end of the tour the royal party took a quick flight home to London. In August the pregnancy was announced and the Duke of Edinburgh took over many of the Queen's official engagements. 'As you realise,' he said in many a speech, 'she has other matters to attend to.'

ABOVE: *Prince Philip wore Court dress and at his left knee, the Order of the Garter at a French banquet, April 1960*

1947   *1957*   *1967*

The Royal Progress

On Friday 19th February 1960 at 3.30pm, the Queen gave birth to their second son at Buckingham Palace. It was the first time that a baby had been born to a *reigning* sovereign since 1857. The birth was the easiest that the Queen had experienced and within hours she was sitting up in bed attending to official papers. Second in line to the throne, taking precedence over Princess Anne, the baby was christened in the Music Room of the Palace and given the names Andrew Albert Christian Edward. The first name had been chosen in honour of the Duke of Edinburgh's father, Prince Andrew of Greece.

Two of the new baby's first visitors were Princess Margaret and the photographer Antony Armstrong-Jones. They had deliberately delayed the announcement of their engagement so as not to overshadow the birth of the Queen and the Duke of Edinburgh's third child. One week later the official announcement was made.

It was noticeable that Prince Andrew was deliberately kept out of the limelight. The Queen and the Duke felt that their two older children had been forced into the public eye too soon. Charles had become withdrawn; Anne was rebellious. Both had suffered from having their mother succeed to the throne so early in their lives. Although the Queen was determined to enjoy her new baby, there was no respite and she returned to official duties three days before the christening, with a state visit by President de Gaulle of France.

TOP: *President de Gaulle and the Duke of Edinburgh drive to review the Household Guards at Horse Guards Parade, April 1960*

BOTTOM: *The Queen and ladies of the Royal Family host President de Gaulle in the Royal box at Covent Garden, April 1960*

1977 *1987* *1997*

The Golden Years

Just before the birth of Prince Andrew the question of the Royal Family's surname had arisen. Were they Windsors, the Queen's maiden name, or should they have Philip's name, Mountbatten ? An official announcement was made that the Royal Family would '... henceforth be called in future generations Mountbatten-Windsor.' The statement concluded: 'The Queen has always wanted, without changing the name of the Royal House established by her grandfather, to associate the name of her husband with her own and his descendants. The Queen has had this in mind for a long time and it is close to her heart.'

The Queen's sister, Princess Margaret, finally married Antony Armstrong-Jones at Westminster Abbey on 6th May 1960. It was the first major royal event to be televised since the Coronation, and far more people owned sets than ever before. *Sunday Night at the London Palladium* had become such a cult, with 20 million viewers, that Churches changed the times of services so as not to clash. In the years that followed, television was to have a marked effect on the way the Royal Family were perceived.

Although the number of invitations declined was said to be unprecedented in a royal wedding, the general public felt sympathetic towards Princess Margaret. Her decision to place royal duty before her own personal happiness with Peter Townsend had cast her in the role of 'tragic' Princess, and there were high hopes that she would enjoy a successful marriage with Antony Armstrong-Jones. Thousands lined the route decorated with pink and white roses for a glimpse of the bride in a stunning Norman Hartnell gown.

Privately the Queen wished to spend more time with her young baby, but was increasingly in demand. In America she was voted the third most admired woman in the world, behind Eleanor Roosevelt and Jackie Kennedy; the British press insisted that she should have headed the list. Prince Philip's popularity, however, was taking a dive.

1947   *1957*   *1967*

The Royal Progress

In January 1961 he and the Queen left England for a tour of Cyprus, India, Nepal, Iran, Turkey and Pakistan. Prince Philip encountered a great deal of criticism, after he, the President of the World Wildlife Fund, shot a tiger through the head. When a royal-watching photographer fell out of a tree in Pakistan, the Prince audibly exclaimed, 'I hope to God he breaks his bloody neck.' In October he made the headlines again after an outspoken speech to British industrialists in which he told them, 'I think it is about time we pulled our fingers out.'

In May 1961 they paid a successful State visit to Italy, meeting Pope John XXIII at the Vatican, and in November defied bomb threats and toured West Africa, including Ghana, Liberia and Sierra Leone. On the tour they were given a two-year-old crocodile as a gift for Prince Andrew. It was kept in the bath of the Queen's Private Secretary, Martin Charteris.

Off-duty the Queen and Prince Philip spent time with their children, often staying at the homes of close friends such as the Beauforts at Badminton House, and relaxed at sporting events. Both enjoyed sport, particularly anything to do with horses, and the Prince relaxed by playing polo. Most summer Saturday afternoons the Queen could be seen at Smith's Lawn, near Windsor Castle, cheering her husband's team. She did not, however, share her husband's passion for sailing and he always attended the annual yachting regatta at Cowes without her; nor did she relish his daredevil exploits in helicopters and gliders. Their interests, although not necessarily the same, have always complimented each other.

ABOVE: *The Queen attends a state banquet during the Royal visit to Persia. L to R: Queen Farah, the Queen, the Shah and Prince Philip, March 1961*

LEFT: *The Queen and Duke of Edinburgh leaving the Taj Mahal on their tour of India, January 1961*

RIGHT: *As the first reigning Monarch for many years to do so, the Queen visits the Pope in the Vatican on the state visit to Italy, May 1961*

1977   1987   1997

The Golden Years

Throughout 1962 Prince Philip tried to modernise the day-today running of Buckingham Palace by employing a Business Efficiency Expert. It was an attempt to cut costs and put an end to some outmoded traditions. Instead of footmen delivering messages by hand, more internal telephones were installed. Over the coming years Prince Philip was to see that the Palace became up-to-date with the latest computer technology.

At the end of July 1962 part of Buckingham Palace was opened to the public for the first time. The private Chapel that had been bombed during the blitz was rebuilt as an art gallery to display treasures from the Royal Collection. Over 200,000 people flocked to see the Queen's paintings in the first year.

In the summer of 1963, while Prince Philip was playing polo at Cowdray Park, the Queen was missing from the opening day of the Goodwood races. Only later was it revealed that she had a doctor's appointment. When in September Buckingham Palace issued the statement that: 'The Queen will undertake no further engagements after Her Majesty leaves Balmoral in October,' it could only mean one thing. By the end of the year it was announced that the Queen, Princess Margaret, Princess Alexandra and the Duchess of Kent were all expecting babies. Antony Armstrong-Jones was elevated to the peerage as the Earl of Snowdon, and Prince Philip once again began to take on more of the Queen's duties. In November he represented his wife at President Kennedy's funeral in Washington. At Christmas Prince Philip joked that Sandringham looked like an ante-natal clinic.

RIGHT: *The Duke of Edinburgh and Prince Charles leave London Airport by car, April 1962*

MIDDLE: *The Queen holding Prince Edward on the train bound to take the Family to Balmoral for the summer holiday, August 1964*

FAR RIGHT: *The Queen inspects a German guard of honour in Bonn, May 1965*

1947   *1957*   *1967*

The Royal Progress

After attending Sir Winston Churchill's State funeral in January 1965, the Queen and the Duke of Edinburgh embarked on a series of visits to non-Commonwealth countries. On their first-ever visit to Ethiopia, their arrival was greeted by a crowd of 200,000. Such was their enthusiasm that the royal procession was frequently brought to a halt. More controversial was a 10 day trip to Germany in May. Now twenty years since the end of the war, it was seen as a sign of reconciliation. It was the first tour of Germany by a British monarch for more than half-a-century. Despite the warmth of the welcome, as the Queen came face-to-face with the Berlin Wall there was no escaping the divisions that still existed within the country.

The Queen gave birth to their fourth child at 8.20pm, on Wednesday 10th March 1964. The boy was christened at Windsor Castle in May and given the names Edward Antony Richard Louis. Elizabeth and Philip's family was now complete. Prince Edward's cousins James Ogilvy, Lady Helen Windsor and Lady Sarah Armstrong-Jones were born to Princess Alexandra, the Duchess of Kent and Princess Margaret respectively that spring, and all now celebrate milestone birthdays at a joint party. Because of the sudden increase in the size of the Royal Family, Christmas at Sandringham appeared overcrowded in 1964 and the following year the festive season was spent at Windsor Castle for the first time.

1977   *1987*   *1997*

The Golden Years

In February 1966 the Queen and Prince Philip said farewell to Prince Charles, who departed for seven months in Australia to broaden his education before going to University. Although he had previously been at Gordonstoun in Scotland, he had kept in close contact with his parents and had been able to see them at Balmoral. Now he was on the other side of the world and the Queen felt the absence of her eldest son deeply.

At home there were problems. During a seaman's strike (16 May - 1 July) the Queen had to sign a proclamation of emergency. It was the first strike of its kind since 1911 and the biggest strike since the war. On an official visit to Belfast in July the Queen and Prince Philip narrowly escaped injury when a concrete slab was dropped on their car. 'It's a strong car,' the Queen said resolutely, but Prime Minister, Harold Wilson, faced questions in the Commons over the Royal Family's security.

1947   *1957*   *1967*

The Royal Progress

On Friday 21st October 1966 an avalanche from an Aberfan coal tip engulfed a school, killing 116 children and 28 adults. One of the worst tragedies Wales had ever known. Not wishing to hinder rescue work, the Queen waited until all hope of finding survivors had gone before she visited the scene of the devastation in South Wales to offer what little comfort was possible to the bereaved. Her very act of concern embedded itself in the hearts of the people. Her face showed the inner grief and compassion that she so obviously felt, and the stark reality before her left a lasting impression. It was one of the most difficult visits of her reign.

FAR LEFT: *The Queen and Dr Franz Meyero ride in open car through the decorated street enroute to Dusseldorf City Hall, on the Royal Tour of Germany, May 1965*

LEFT: *Derby Day at Epsom, May 1966*

1977   *1987*   *1997*

57

The Golden Years

By February 1967 Elizabeth had been Queen for fifteen years. That year she opened the Queen Elizabeth Hall on the South Bank of the River Thames, launched the *QE2* liner at Clydebank and, with echoes of Elizabeth I, knighted Sir Francis Chichester who had sailed around the world in 107 days. Yet one event stood out in people's minds more than any other. For the first time since the abdication crisis of 1936, the Queen and the Queen Mother publicly met the Duke and Duchess of Windsor. Had Edward VIII not relinquished the throne for the divorcee Wallis Simpson, Elizabeth would never have become Queen.

ABOVE: *The Daily Mail reporting of the historic meeting between the Queen and the Duke and Duchess of Windsor, June 8, 1967*

LEFT: *On the balcony at Buckingham Palace for the Trooping of the Colour. L to R: Prince Edward, the Queen, Duke of Edinburgh and Princess Anne. June 1967*

TOP RIGHT: *Prince Philip led his team to victory playing polo on a bicycle at a spur-of-the-moment match at Smith's Lawn, Windsor, August 1967*

BOTTOM RIGHT: *The Queen attends the premiere of 'Doctor Doolittle' at the Odeon, Marble Arch. L to R: Joan Collins, Anthony Newley, Mrs Richard Attenborough, December 1967*

1947   1957   1967

The Royal Progress

On 7th June 1967 a memorial plaque in memory of Queen Mary was unveiled at Marlborough House by the Queen. The Duke of Windsor was invited as Queen Mary's eldest son. It was a tense occasion for all concerned and all eyes noted that the former Wallis Simpson did not curtsey. Prince Philip's expression showed mixed emotion as the Duke of Windsor exchanged a formal kiss with the Queen.

At the close of a difficult year, the Queen and Prince Philip returned to Malta to open Parliament. Within days of their 20th wedding anniversary, it was a nostalgic return to the country that held happy memories of the carefree days of their early married life.

1977   *1987*   *1997*

1947   1957   1967

THE 67-77
The Silver Years
ROYAL DECADE

1977   1987   1997

The Golden Years

1967 - 1977
The Silver Years

Despite Prince Philip's attempts to modernise the internal administration of the Royal Family's daily lives, by the late 1960's there were external mutterings that the monarchy was in danger of becoming an anachronism.

In a period of great social change, with unprecedented advances in science, medicine, and technology that could even place a man on the moon for the first time, it became essential for the Royal Family to adapt. A fine line had to be drawn between tradition and keeping pace with the times. In the end, the perfect balance was found which gave the monarchy a renewed popularity.

When the Queen struck the first decimal coin at the Royal Mint in 1968, it seemed symbolic of a move forward. Just as an up-to-date portrait of the Queen would appear on the changing coins of the realm, so a new light was to be cast on Her Majesty's family. For the first time ever, the Queen and Prince Philip allowed themselves to be followed by a film crew for an entire year. From 8th June, 1968, to 18th May, 1969, more than 43 hours of film were taken of them, both in private and public, to produce the ground-breaking documentary *Royal Family*. Richard Cawston's film was an attempt to show the human side of royalty, both at work and play.

PREVIOUS PAGE: *The Queen and Prince Philip on their Silver Wedding anniversary, November 1977*

LEFT: *The Queen, Prince Philip and Prince Charles attend a gala performance of 'The Mikado' at the Saville Theatre in London, February 1968*

RIGHT: *The Queen, Prince Philip and Princess Anne arrive for a preview of the ITV series on The Life of Earl Mountbatten of Burma, December 1968*

1947   1957   1967

The Silver Years

MILESTONES

1967
The Queen launched the liner Queen Elizabeth 2 at Clydebank

1969
Prince of Wales's 21st birthday

1970
First 'walkabout' in England

1972
National celebrations for the Queen and Duke of Edinburgh's Silver Wedding Anniversary

1976
The Queen celebrated her 50th birthday at Windsor Castle

1977 1987 1997

The Golden Years

For many, the 110 minute film offered a rare glimpse of the surprisingly homely Royal apartments. Following their working lives, it became apparent that although Prince Philip was frequently seen on engagements with the Queen, he actually had a very full diary of his own, with over 400 patronages. A lover of outdoor activities, and having launched his own Award Scheme to encourage initiative and adventure, he was shown piloting a helicopter to fulfil official duties. From hosting a Diplomatic Reception at Buckingham Palace to undertaking a State Visit to South America, the documentary gave an insight into the packed working life of the Queen and Prince Philip. Yet, for the 23 million viewers who watched the broadcast in June 1969, it was the off-duty moments that elicited the greatest interest. The Queen driving a car and taking Prince Edward shopping; she and Prince Philip decorating the Christmas tree with their children at Windsor and cooking a barbeque at Balmoral. For the general public, the documentary was a milestone in broadcasting. For the cynics, too much daylight had been let in upon Royal workings, so eroding the mysteries inherent to the monarchy. Having prised Pandora's box ajar, it would be impossible to close the lid completely.

LEFT: *The Queen with her four corgis; Heather, Buzz, Foxy and Tiny, February 1968*

RIGHT: *The Queen presenting the new Prince of Wales after his Investiture, July 1969*

1947 *1957* *1967*

64

The Silver Years

A week after *Royal Family* had been broadcast, the Queen invested Prince Charles as the 21st Prince of Wales in a colourful ceremony at Caernarfon Castle on 1st July 1969. Ancient though the pageant appeared to be, no specific ceremony existed until 1911 when one was created for Edward (later Duke of Windsor). Prince Charles's Investiture combined modern spectacle with medieval splendour. Beneath a state-of-the-art Perspex canopy in the thirteenth-century castle precincts, the Queen placed a contemporary style crown on the Prince's head with ancient words straight out of Arthurian legend. 'I, Charles Prince of Wales, do become your liege man of life and limb and of earthly worship, and faith and truth I will bear unto you to live and die against all manner of folks.' When rehearsing for the Investiture the Prince of Wales's crown slipped over his eyes and, although it was reduced in size for the actual day, the Queen later confessed that she had almost laughed during the ceremony as she placed it on her son's head.

1977   *1987*   *1997*

The Golden Years

LEFT: *The Queen places the Coronet on the head of Prince Charles during the Investiture ceremony, July 1969*

BELOW: *The Duke of Edinburgh sits in the driving seat of a British 50-ton Chieftain tank at Gallows Hills. He drove the tank and fired its 120mm gun, March 1969*

RIGHT: *The Duke of Edinburgh and Princess Anne yachting at Cowes, August 1970*

The Investiture attracted 200,000,000 television viewers worldwide and ensured that the Royal Family's popularity was as high as in Coronation year. Not only did Prince Charles take centre stage, but 1969 was the year that Princess Anne began undertaking royal duties. To prevent nerves, the first engagement was sprung on her at the last minute when the Duke of Edinburgh surprisingly found that his diary had been double booked. Concerned that the public might have had a surfeit of the Royal Family on television in 1969, the Queen did not make her annual Christmas Day broadcast. Such an outcry ensued that the tradition was revived in 1970 by public demand.

1947   1957   1967

The Silver Years

Although a successful year, for the Duke of Edinburgh there was private grief when his mother died suddenly at Buckingham Palace. A woman of great character, Princess Alice had been born deaf and spent much of her life working quietly for the poor and sick. Wearing a nun's habit, she was able to go about her work unrecognised and spent the last two years of her life living at Buckingham Palace so that the Queen and Duke of Edinburgh could see her daily.

In complete contrast, the Queen Mother continued to live a very active public life and national celebrations were held for her 70th birthday. Along with two other members of the family - Henry, Duke of Gloucester and Earl Mountbatten of Burma - she was born with the century and all attended a special family party.

Following the unveiling of Annigoni's controversial portrait of the Queen at the National Portrait Gallery, said to lack the dignity of his more famous 1954 'blue' painting, the Queen and Prince Philip paid an official visit to Australia and New Zealand. Whereas in the past the royal couple had always been driven through the waiting crowds in open topped cars, they now broke with tradition and initiated the 'walkabout'. Although they had walked along streets in Malta talking to people in November 1967, as the Queen Mother had done before them informally on a visit to Canada before the war, this was the first *organised* 'walkabout'. Thus, on 3 May 1970, the people of New Zealand were delighted to be able to talk to the Queen and the Duke, shake hands, present gifts and take close-up photographs, in an unprecedented fashion. Pleased with the response to this new accessibility, the Queen and Prince Philip repeated the exercise in Britain while on a visit to Coventry in June. It was to become an expected feature of any Royal visit from then onwards.

1977   *1987*   *1997*

The Golden Years

With their two elder children having reached their majority, the Queen and Prince Philip became increasingly proud of their exploits. In August 1971 Prince Philip went to RAF Cranwell to watch Prince Charles being awarded his flying wings after a five month course at Cranwell. The following month Princess Anne, having that year accepted the patronage of the Save the Children Fund, made equestrian history by winning the European Horse Trials at Burghley. The Queen and the Duke of Edinburgh watched anxiously from the stands as the Princess on 'Doublet' encountered the 12 fences that stood between her and the European crown. Glued to television sets throughout the country, thousands of viewers 'rode' with her every inch of the way to victory.

Suddenly the little followed sport of eventing became known throughout the world. The BBC heralded Princess Anne as Sports Personality of the Year after millions had voted for her, and *The Daily Express* named her as Sportswoman of 1971. One of the Princess's rivals at the Badminton Horse Trials that year was an officer cadet called Mark Phillips.

1947   *1957*   *1967*

The Silver Years

Throughout her reign Queen Elizabeth II has always been anxious to avoid controversy, even if Prince Philip has been unafraid of speaking his mind. In October 1971, however, the Queen was placed in an uncomfortable position when Emperor Hirohito of Japan visited Britain for the first time since the Second World War. Former prisoners of war called for a boycott of Japanese products in protest at Hirohito's visit and although a large crowd lined the streets to watch the carriage procession to Buckingham Palace, there was no cheering. 'We cannot pretend that the past did not exist,' said the Queen diplomatically. 'We cannot pretend that relations between our two peoples have always been peaceful and friendly.' As with her visit to Germany, she and Prince Philip hoped that they had in some small way begun the process of reconciliation.

LEFT: *Prince Philip watches his son receive his pilot's wings at a passing out parade at Cranwell, the RAF college in Lincolnshire, August 1971*

RIGHT: *The Queen leaps ashore from pontoon to Dolmabache Palace Jetty after disembarking from the 'Britannia' on Royal visit to Turkey, October 1971*

1977   *1987*   *1997*

The Golden Years

Within her own family the Queen had equally attempted to sweeten the bitterness caused by Edward VIII's abdication. Although her life had been permanently changed as a result of the King's decision to relinquish the throne, she had been but ten years old in 1936 and bore the Duke of Windsor no animosity. At the end of May 1972 she and Prince Philip visited him at his Paris home, aware that he had cancer of the throat. The Duke died eight days later at the age of 77. His body was flown back to England and lay in state for two days at St. George's Chapel, Windsor, where 60,000 mourners filed past. The Duchess of Windsor came to England for the Duke's funeral and stayed at Buckingham Palace as the Queen's guest. She flew back to Paris from Heathrow, and boarded the plane without even a backward glance at the country her husband had given up for her.

1972 was a year when the Queen and the Duke of Edinburgh could not avoid looking back to the past, as they celebrated their Silver Wedding Anniversary on 20th November. They returned to Westminster Abbey for a service of thanksgiving, joined by other couples who had been married on the same day twenty-five years earlier. A carriage procession to the Guildhall followed for a luncheon with the Lord Mayor of London. 'I think everybody really will concede,' began the Queen afterwards, 'that on this, of all days, I should begin my speech with the words *my husband and I*.' By poking fun at her own catch-phrase, she received a standing ovation. Prince Philip looked on in amusement.

ABOVE: *Thanksgiving Service for the Silver Wedding Anniversary at Westminster Abbey. L to R: Lady Sarah Armstrong-Jones, Viscount Linley, Princess Margaret, Prince Edward, Queen Mother, Prince Andrew, Princess Anne and the Prince of Wales. November 1972*

1947   *1957*   *1967*

The Silver Years

'A marriage begins by joining man and wife together,' the Queen continued, 'but this relationship between two people, however deep at the time, needs to develop and mature with the passing years... When the Bishop was asked about sin, he replied with simple conviction that he was against it. If I am asked today what I think about family life after twenty-five years of marriage, I can answer with equal simplicity and conviction. I am for it.'

That afternoon the Queen and Duke of Edinburgh went on a walkabout through the Barbican area of London, and returned in a carriage procession to Buckingham Palace for a private family dinner at which Prince Charles had arranged for the wedding march to be played.

LEFT: *The Silver Wedding Edition front page of The Daily Mail, November 1972*

BELOW: *Walkabout at the Barbican, November 1972*

1977   1987   1997

The Golden Years

In 1973 the Queen and Prince Philip were back at Westminster Abbey again for the wedding of their only daughter, Princess Anne, to Captain Mark Phillips of the Dragoon Guards. In spite having been thrown off her horse 'Goodwill' at the European Championships in Kiev, chipping her shoulder-bone, Princess Anne looked radiant on her wedding day in a Tudor-inspired dress and the fringe tiara worn by the Queen on her own wedding day. Although a London store had claimed that it would have a copy of the wedding dress on sale within hours, Susan Small's intricate Elizabethan design proved impossible to reproduce.

The wedding day itself - 14th November - coincided with Prince Charles's twenty-fifth birthday. The wedding ring was made from the same nugget of Welsh gold that had been used for the rings of both the Queen and the Queen Mother, and in Anne's bouquet was a sprig of myrtle from a tree descended from the myrtle in Queen Victoria's bridal bouquet. Although the wedding was classed as a family affair and not a state occasion, it was declared a national holiday and 500 million television viewers watched the ceremony. The following day the newspapers focused on the Queen. As a monarch, with the eyes of the world media upon her, she had not been allowed the luxury of a mother's tear at her daughter's marriage.

The Queen and the Duke of Edinburgh delighted in visiting Anne and Mark in their first marital home - Oak Grove Lodge at Sandhurst - and took along practical presents for the kitchen.

The following spring, however, their worst nightmare happened when an attempt was made to kidnap Princess Anne. The Queen and Prince Philip were on an official visit to Java on 20th March 1974, unaware of the drama that was unfolding within yards of Buckingham Palace.

LEFT: *Little Shona Beaton amuses a Royal at the Investitive, Buckingham Palace, November 1974*

RIGHT: *The Queen opens the Olympic games, July 1976*

1947   1957   1967

The Silver Years

Returning home from a Riding for the Disabled Association engagement, the car containing Princess Anne and Captain Phillips was stopped by a crazed gunman in an attempt to kidnap the Queen's only daughter and hold her to ransom for three-million pounds. The gunman, 26-year-old Ian Ball, fired straight into the royal car, narrowly missing Captain Phillips, before attempting to forcibly drag Princess Anne out, ripping the sleeve of her blue velvet dress. In the ensuing struggle, he shot the Princess's bodyguard in the chest, stomach and hand; fired at the chauffeur from point-blank range; shot a policeman in the stomach and a journalist, who got out of his car to help, in the chest.

The Queen and Prince Philip were told of the incident by telephone once the Princess was safe. Shaken but undaunted, Anne drove herself home to Sandhurst, with one concession, an armed detective in the front seat. Late for a dinner party with friends, the Princess calmly apologised - 'We got held up,' she said.

As a result of the kidnap attempt security around the Royal Family noticeably tightened. Over the ensuing years, the Queen and Prince Philip were to find their public and private lives increasingly hampered by security arrangements. The Queen had been protected all her life, but close friends described Prince Philip as feeling like a caged bird.

To provide greater privacy for their daughter and son-in-law, the Queen purchased Gatcombe Park. A Gloucestershire country house set in 530 acres, Gatcombe was leased to the couple and the surrounding farmland enabled Captain Phillips to pursue a career in agriculture.

While Princess Anne's marriage appeared to be a success, Princess Margaret's had begun to founder. Many blamed her marital problems on the fact that she had not been allowed to marry Peter Townsend. After much speculation, an announcement was made from Kensington Palace in March 1976 that Princess Margaret and Lord Snowdon were to separate. The Princess, who had been forbidden to marry a divorced man, was to become a divorcee herself.

On 21st April 1976 the Queen celebrated her 50th birthday quietly with Prince Philip at Windsor. Frequently wined and dined on a grand scale by the very nature of their position, they prefer to mark family anniversaries simply, given the choice. With plans for the Silver Jubilee celebrations already in hand for 1977, the Queen was determined not to over egg the pudding.

1977   *1987*   *1997*

73

The Golden Years

LEFT: *The Queen leaves Windsor Chapel in Windsor Great Park after a service to commemorate the 25th anniversary of her accession to the throne. Accompanying the Queen are Prince Philip, Prince Charles, Princess Anne, Prince Edward, Princess Margaret and the Queen Mother, February 1977*

That summer, the Queen and Prince Philip paid a State Visit to America, arriving in Washington on 7th July for their bicentennial celebrations. For them, the highlight of the tour was a visit to Canada ten days later where the Queen officially opened the Olympic Games. For the first time, their own daughter was taking part. Although the Princess insisted on being treated like her fellow competitors, travelling economy class and queuing at the buffet for her meals, Anne was the only female not to be given a sex test. Princess Anne's overall performance was disappointing in the three-day event; coming 26th in the dressage, she was knocked unconscious in front of her parents during the cross-country, and came fourth in the show jumping.

After a twenty-five year reign, the Queen and Prince Philip were used to a full and exhausting itinerary, but 1977 was to prove one of the most demanding years they had ever experienced. Great Britain and the rest of the Commonwealth celebrated the Queen's Silver Jubilee with more verve and enthusiasm than anyone could ever have imagined.

The year began quietly enough for the Queen and the Duke at Sandringham. On 6th February they attended a simple private Church service at Windsor to mark the twenty-fifth anniversary to the day of the Queen's accession. Three days later they left Heathrow airport for the first tour of the season. Visiting Samoa, Tonga, Fiji, New Zealand, Australia and Papua New Guinea, by the end of Jubilee year the Queen and Prince Philip would have visited almost every country of the Commonwealth, travelling some 56,000 miles.

1947 *1957* *1967*

The Silver Years

Back home, every region of the United Kingdom was to receive a visit from their Monarch too, beginning with a tour of Scotland. With talk of Scottish devolution, the Queen had unexpectedly warned Parliament of her objections to the break up of the United Kingdom.

'I number Kings and Queens of England *and* of Scotland *and* Princes of Wales amongst my ancestors. I cannot forget that I was crowned Queen of the United Kingdom of Great Britain and Northern Ireland. Perhaps this Jubilee is a time to remind ourselves of the benefits which union has conferred, at home and in our international dealings, on the inhabitants of all parts of this United Kingdom.'

As the royal train approached Glasgow Central station there were fears that the Queen and the Duke might receive a hostile reception, yet, as the sun broke through the clouds, more than a quarter of a million people gave them an enthusiastic welcome.

An enthusiasm that was repeated throughout the eleven day tour. After a visit to the General Assembly of the Church of Scotland in Edinburgh, a man shouted out 'Will ye no come back again?', and immediately everyone present began singing spontaneously.

BELOW: *The Royal party at Ascot, June 1977*

1977   *1987*   *1997*

The Golden Years

On 6th June the Queen lit the first of a chain of 102 bonfires that spread from Windsor to the Shetland Islands to signal the start of a full week of Jubilee Celebrations. A torch lit by the Queen was flown to Sydney to set off a further 3000 bonfires across Australia.

For Jubilee Day itself, some five million extra tourists poured into London and street parties were held in every town and village in the British Isles. The Queen and Prince Philip drove in the Gold State Coach, which had taken them to her Coronation 24 years earlier, to a Thanksgiving Service in St. Paul's Cathedral. To see if the coach could make the difficult journey through the narrow streets to St. Paul's, it was given a trial run in November 1976 at 4 o'clock one morning.

RIGHT: *Service at St. Paul's Cathedral for the Silver Jubilee, June 1977*

1947   *1957*   *1967*

The Silver Years

RIGHT: *The River Pageant and Tour, part of the Silver Jubilee celebrations. The Queen meets the people at St. Katherine's Dock, June 1977*

BELOW: *St. Katherine's Dock. A salute from young sailors who tied up their dinghies,*

At St.Paul's Cathedral with a congregation of 2,700 and 500 million television viewers worldwide, the Archbishop of Canterbury spoke of the monarchy as something 'at the heart of our national life of incalculable value.' After the service the Queen, dressed in a rose-pink outfit that had been seen the previous July when she opened the Olympic Games in Montreal, and the Duke of Edinburgh in naval uniform, went on a walkabout to the Guildhall to attend a Lord Mayor's Banquet. 'When I was twenty-one I pledged my life to the service of our people,' the Queen concluded her speech that day, 'and I asked for God's help to make good that vow. Although that vow was made in my salad days, when I was green in judgment, I do not regret nor retract one word of it.'

After a carriage drive back to Buckingham Palace, the Queen and Prince Philip appeared on the balcony three times as more than a million people thronged into The Mall to show their loyalty and appreciation.

1977   *1987*   *1997*

The Golden Years

LEFT: *Part of the River Pageant and Tours, the Queen at Greenwich, June 1977*

BELOW: *Review of the army at Sennelafer, Germany, Silver Jubilee, July 1977*

In the week that followed, the Queen and the Duke of Edinburgh made a triumphal procession along the River Thames, the historic route for royal pageantry, to Greenwich. Officially called the 'River Progress', it was one of the Jubilee's longest days, with more than twelve hours of non-stop events for the Queen and her husband 'Baron Greenwich'. The day ended with a firework display over the river, and when the couple eventually arrived back at Buckingham Palace, so great was the crowd that they had to bow to the chanting and shortly after midnight came out onto the balcony, to everyone's satisfaction.

1947   *1957*   *1967*

The Silver Years

The remainder of Jubilee Year saw the Queen and the Duke of Edinburgh visiting their realms and territories in a punishing schedule. From a tour of Wales to an historic visit to Northern Ireland, they travelled widely throughout Britain, before resuming visits to Commonwealth countries - Canada, Bahamas, the Virgin Islands, Antigua, and Barbados - flying home on *Concorde*.

Five days before their thirtieth wedding anniversary, the Queen was unexpectedly late for an investiture ceremony at Buckingham Palace. She arrived in high spirits and announced that her first grandchild - Peter Phillips - had just been born. It was an appropriate personal note on which to close a year of celebration.

ABOVE: *The Queen meets cubs at Greenwich as part of the Silver Jubilee celebrations, June 1977*

1977   1987   1997

1947 *1957* *1967*

THE
77-87
Dawn of a Dynasty
ROYAL DECADE

1977 1987 1997

The Golden Years

1977 - 1987
Dawn of a Dynasty

The success of the Silver Jubilee took even the Queen and the Duke of Edinburgh by surprise. They had undertaken the most extensive programme of engagements in twenty-five years and had received overwhelming outpourings of affection. In London alone there were 4,000 street parties and the Queen appeared to symbolise national unity.

After a year in which she was feted as a popular monarch, the focus began to change. Now that they were grandparents for the first time, the spotlight narrowed in on the *family* life of the Queen and Prince Philip. The Jubilee had offered an excuse to look back over the reign; it was inevitable that the public would now want to look forward. In the next generation lay the future of the House of Windsor.

Having once made the mistake of saying that thirty was a good age to marry, rumours of an imminent engagement dogged Prince Charles and dominated the gossip columns throughout 1978. His name was linked particularly with Princess Marie-Astrid of Luxembourg and Lady Sarah Spencer, although not her younger sister Diana.

Prince Andrew celebrated his eighteenth birthday on 19th February 1978 and became eligible for a £17,262 allowance from the Civil List. Ever thrifty, the Queen decided that only £8,000 was needed for public duties and the remainder was invested for the future. With dashing good looks, Prince Andrew followed in his father's footsteps by entering the Royal Naval College at Dartmouth, and in 1980 joined the Navy for training as a helicopter pilot.

PREVIOUS PAGE: *President and Mrs Ronald Reagan with the Queen and Duke of Edinburgh at Windsor, June 1982*

RIGHT: *The Queen and Prince Philip posing for an official picture with Col. Commandant General Sir Victor Fitzgeorge-Balfour at the presentation of new colours to the Honourable Artillery Company at Armoury House, London June 1980.*

1947   *1957*   *1967*

Dawn of a Dynasty

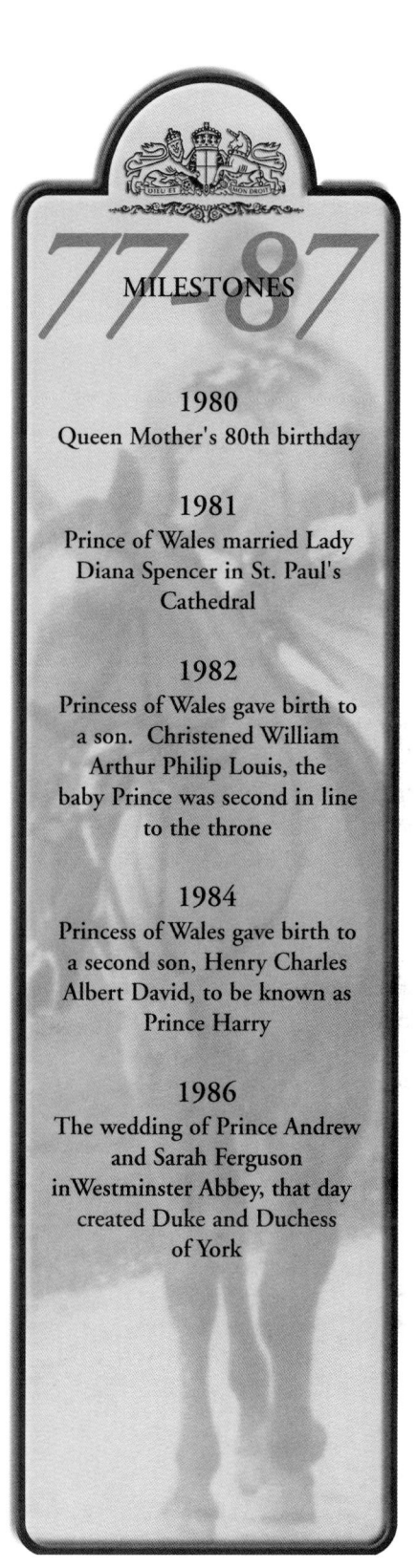

77-87 MILESTONES

1980
Queen Mother's 80th birthday

1981
Prince of Wales married Lady Diana Spencer in St. Paul's Cathedral

1982
Princess of Wales gave birth to a son. Christened William Arthur Philip Louis, the baby Prince was second in line to the throne

1984
Princess of Wales gave birth to a second son, Henry Charles Albert David, to be known as Prince Harry

1986
The wedding of Prince Andrew and Sarah Ferguson in Westminster Abbey, that day created Duke and Duchess of York

1977   *1987*   *1997*

The Golden Years

Princess Anne was travelling widely and started to visit some of the poorest regions of the world as President of the Save the Children Fund. At times ill-tempered in public, her volatile reactions frequently overshadowed her achievements. Only when she had mellowed did the public take Anne to their hearts.

Receiving far less publicity, Prince Edward was studying at Gordonstoun, Prince Philip's old school. Working for a place at Jesus College, Cambridge, his goal was to join the Royal Marines. With their children apparently settled, it was business as usual for the Queen and Prince Philip.

LEFT: *The Queen with the King of Saudi Arabia upon arrival during the tour of the Middle East, February 1979*

RIGHT: *In respectful dress, the Queen greets a line up of princes in Riyadh,*

1947   1957   1967

Dawn of a Dynasty

Overseas tours continued to be an important part of their work, promoting friendly relations and strengthening economic ties. Even after thirty years experience as a working couple, foreign visits still continued to present challenges. In February 1979 the Queen and Prince Philip undertook a three week tour of the Middle East, visiting Bahrain, Kuwait, Saudi Arabia, Qatar, the United Arab Emirates and Oman. The Queen was welcomed to Saudi Arabia as an 'Honorary Man' and her clothes had to follow a strict code. No flesh of the arms, legs or neck was to be revealed, so the Queen had a number of full-length dresses designed that could be easily shortened on her return home for further use.

1977   *1987*   *1997*

85

The Golden Years

On 17th October, the Queen and Prince Philip paid a State Visit to Italy and met Pope John Paul II, before moving on to Morocco. Here the Queen gave one of the few public displays of emotion by tapping her foot in anger at being kept waiting in a tent for nearly an hour in the hot desert by her host, King Hassan. Worried about security, the King continually changed the itinerary at the last minute. 'We have been especially touched by the way in which Your Majesty took such a personal interest in our programme ... ' said the Queen with a rare touch of sarcasm. Privately, members of the Household classed the tour as the least successful State Visit ever.

On 24th February 1981 the Queen and Prince Philip were happier to announce that the Prince of Wales was to marry Lady Diana Spencer. News of the engagement soon had the world gripped by Di-mania with everything from her hairstyle to her flat shoes copied. It was the biggest boost that the fashion trade had known for decades with distinctive 'Diana' feathered hats, pie-crust collars and even copies of her sapphire and diamond engagement ring selling by the thousand. Within weeks the shy 19 year old became the most photographed girl in the world, hailed by the press as the perfect marriage partner, with 'a history but no past'. With no skeletons in the cupboard and the daughter of an Earl, 'Lady Di' seemed ideal material for a future Queen.

1947   *1957*   *1967*

Dawn of a Dynasty

Hailed as the wedding of the decade and the first marriage of a monarch's immediate heir since the Queen's own in 1947, the ceremony took place at St. Paul's Cathedral on 29th July 1981. Diana became the fairy-tale Princess, taken to her wedding in a glass coach. The wedding dress created by Elizabeth and David Emanuel was greeted with mixed reaction. The magic confection of satin, lace and shimmering mother of pearl was not everyone's choice for the young bride.

'Why make someone with a figure like *Concorde* look like a battleship?' grumbled one MP. Seen by millions throughout the world, the ceremony was not without hitches. Lady Diana mixed up the names of her future husband, calling him 'Philip'. 'She's just married my father!' roared Prince Andrew afterwards. Prince Charles stumbled too, offering to share 'All *thy* worldly goods...'

In her bridal bouquet the new Princess of Wales had some yellow 'Lord Mountbatten' roses. As the couple came out on to the balcony of Buckingham Palace later in the day, the Queen and the Duke of Edinburgh stood out of sight chatting. Suddenly they became aware of chanting in The Mall. 'We want the Queen!' came the cry, and she and Prince Philip emerged to cheers as they had done on their own wedding day nearly 35 years before.

LEFT: *The wedding of Prince Charles and Lady Diana Spencer after their marriage appearing on the balcony of Buckingham Palace, July 1981*

RIGHT: *The newly married couple leave the Cathedral*

1977   *1987*   *1997*

The Golden Years

The Queen was justifiably angry by the lack of security and that she should have been subjected to such an ordeal. Fagan was harmless enough, but had he been a terrorist the Queen could quite literally have been murdered in her own bed. A week later she went into hospital for the first time in her life to have a wisdom tooth removed, and returned home to find that her personal bodyguard had been forced to resign due to a scandal. With the death of a close personal friend, Lord Rupert Nevill, once Prince Philip's Private Secretary, and an IRA outrage that killed eleven men of the Household Cavalry and seven horses, July 1982 was one of the most distressing months of the Queen's reign.

The strain of the year had begun when their second son, Prince Andrew, took part in the Falklands conflict. His helicopter was used as a decoy for exocet missiles fired by Argentinian jets. The Queen was involved in four ways: as Sovereign of the Falkland Islands; Head of the Commonwealth; Head of the Armed Forces and as a mother. By the time the conflict came to an end, nearly 1,000 servicemen and civilians from Great Britain and Argentina had lost their lives. On 16th September a very relieved Queen and Prince Philip welcomed their son home in an emotional reunion on board his ship *HMS Invincible*. Later the Royal Family attended a Falklands Service in St. Paul's Cathedral.

The high point of 1982 for the Queen and the Duke came on 21st June when the Princess of Wales gave birth to a son. Later christened William Arthur Philip Louis, the baby was second in line to the throne. Two years later a second son and heir, Henry Charles Albert David, known as 'Prince Harry' was born on 15th September. The future of the Mountbatten-Windsor dynasty was assured.

Over the year the Queen visibly aged, but after their annual holiday at Balmoral where she and Philip seem most able to relax, they embarked on the usual full diary of engagements. Making over 1,000 official visits each year between them, neither the Queen nor the Duke had any intention of cutting back. In the Autumn of 1982 they set off on yet another lengthy tour, starting in Australia where Prince Philip opened the 12th Commonwealth Games in Brisbane and the Queen later performed the closing ceremony, before a tour of Pacific Islands.

LEFT: *The return of HMS Invincible from the Falklands, September 1992*

RIGHT: *A bit of family fun is captured on film as Princess Anne mimes a drink for her parents while watching racing at Epsom, June 1982*

1947   *1957*   *1967*

Dawn of a Dynasty

The Golden Years

Dawn of a Dynasty

FAR LEFT: *The Queen and Duke with President and Mrs Ronald Reagan at Windsor, June 1982*

LEFT: *The Queen and Diana watch Charles play polo at Windsor, July, 1984*

Visiting Tuvalu, Fiji, Kiribati, Nauru, Papua New Guinea and the Solomon Islands, the Queen and the Duke were seen experiencing a new culture. They drank from coconut shells and were faced with vast banquets of local delicacies including cooked blackbirds and bats. Prince Philip sampled while the Queen watched. Neither could contain their laughter when both were consecutively crowned with floral headdresses. Arriving in Tuvalu the Queen and the Prince looked slightly nervous as they were each rowed ashore in tiny canoes; looks turned to bemusement when they were lifted up to shoulder height and carried through the streets.

Three months later, in February 1983, they began the most extensive tour of the Western hemisphere they had ever made, visiting Jamaica, the Cayman Islands (where 75,000 stamps and 20,000 coins were produced to commemorate the occasion), Mexico, the United States and Canada. In America they experienced the worst weather ever known on a royal tour and had to abandon part of the itinerary because of fierce gales. When they met President Reagan for lunch at his ranch, the Queen was forced to don raincoat and boots as the heavens opened.

On 2nd March the Royal party were forced to book into an hotel rather than return to *Britannia* at sea. 'I knew before we came that we had exported many of our traditions to the USA,' said the Queen in her deadpan fashion, 'but I had not realised that the weather was one of them.' In spite of the weather, American interest in the Queen and the Duke had not waned and at one point 3,300 pressmen followed the couple, with 40 television cameras from different channels.

1977   *1987*   *1997*

The Golden Years

Back home, the couple continued to fulfil a punishing schedule, undertaking both separate and joint engagements. It was noticeable that when the Duke of Edinburgh was working solo that he tended to be more controversial than being in the presence of his wife. Paying a visit to Los Angeles as President of the World Wildlife Fund, he spoke surrounded by crocodile handbags and ivory carvings. In an impassioned speech he tried to encourage rich Californians to stop buying products that caused animal deaths.

LEFT: *The Queen and Duke of Edinburgh remembering Armistice Day in East Africa, November 1983*

RIGHT: *The Queen and Mrs Indira Ghandi at Delhi Airport at the start of the Queen and Duke's ten day tour of India, November 1983*

1947   *1957*   *1967*

Dawn of a Dynasty

In April 1983 the Prince attended a symposium in London on the dangers of nuclear weapons. 'Many people still fervently believe that wars are created by weapons,' he said. 'What really matters are the scruples of their possessors. People are far more dangerous than inanimate objects.' His overall view was that nuclear weapons act as an important deterrent and discourage 'armed conflict in Europe', a view which earned him criticism for not retaining Royal neutrality - criticism lobbied at the Prince Consort 130 years before when he had expressed personal views.

Off-duty, Prince Philip gave up polo in the 1980's and took up carriage driving instead. In 1985 the world pairs championship was held at Sandringham where the Prince established a Carriage Driving Centre. The Queen prefers him carriage driving to playing polo, considering it to be less hazardous, and takes an interest in the breeding of his horses. In the 1980's she still nursed an ambition herself - that one of her own horses should one day win the Derby. On occasions she has paid private visits to America to purchase good quality stud horses, bred for their stamina and speed.

1977   *1987*   *1997*

The Golden Years

A month later, on 6th June, the Queen and Prince Philip flew to Normandy in a red Wessex helicopter of the Queen's Flight for the 40th Anniversary of D-Day. Joined by King Olav of Norway, Queen Beatrix of the Netherlands, King Baudouin of Belgium and Prince Jean, Grand Duke of Luxembourg, they visited the Commonwealth War Graves at Bayeux, being met at the gates of the cemetery by President Mitterrand of France and President Reagan of the United States. With 10,000 war veterans present, the Heads of State laid wreaths in memory of those who gave their lives for their country. Later, eight Heads of State, including Premier Trudeau of Canada, walked on Utah Beach, the site of the D-Day landings and the scene of some of the toughest fighting of the war. 'We are proud,' said the Queen. 'We cannot and will not forget those who are no longer with us. May they rest in peace.' The Queen and Prince Philip ended the day with a quiet dinner on *Britannia*.

1947   *1957*   *1967*

Dawn of a Dynasty

LEFT: *The Queen with a three year old Zara Phillips on her knee at Smith's Lawn, Windsor, June 1984*

RIGHT: *The Queen with Prince Philip as he prepares for the National Carriage Driving Championships at Windsor Great Park, September 1984*

1977   1987   1997

The Golden Years

More overseas visits followed. In March 1985 they paid the first State Visit to Portugal since 1957, and in October visited ten Caribbean countries in 26 days - the climax of which was a gathering of Heads of Government for the Commonwealth Conference in the Bahamas. At a banquet on the Royal Yacht, the Queen was kept waiting over an hour for several guests, including India's Rajiv Gandhi, who had decided to travel by boat and were delayed by a sudden squall.

In February 1986 the Queen and the Duke of Edinburgh visited Nepal, New Zealand and Australia. A successful tour with the largest crowds the Queen had ever encountered in Australia, causing Neville Wran the chairman of the ruling Labour Party to admit: 'Australia will not become a Republic - at least not in my lifetime and it will take a braver man than me to raise that subject again.'

Despite her popularity, the Queen became a victim of Maori demonstrations in New Zealand. As she toured Ellerslie racetrack in Auckland two girls threw eggs at the royal car, hitting the Queen. It was the first time she had been hit by a missile in her 34 year reign. At a banquet that evening Her Majesty joked that she preferred her eggs for breakfast.

1947   *1957*   *1967*

Dawn of a Dynasty

LEFT: *The Queen and Commonwealth leaders attending a summit at Buckingham Palace.*
L to R: Bob Hawke, Margaret Thatcher, Sir Lynden Pindling, the Queen, Kenneth Kaunda, Shridath Ramphal, Rajiv Gandhi and Robert Mugabe August 1986

BELOW: *The Royal Family watch Prince Andrew and Sarah Ferguson leave Westminster Abbey, July 1986*

On their return home, following weeks of speculation, Buckingham Palace announced the engagement of Prince Andrew to Miss Sarah Ferguson, the second daughter of Prince Charles's polo manager. Prince Andrew and 26 year old 'Fergie', as she was dubbed, had known each other since the age of four, the Fergusons being related to the Royal Family through Princess Alice, Duchess of Gloucester, a cousin of Sarah's father.

The wedding took place on 23rd July 1986, and opinions about 'Fergie's' suitability as a royal bride were divided. 'Like a breath of fresh air,' said some about the boisterous fun-lover. 'Vulgar, vulgar, vulgar,' thought others. Ninety minutes before the wedding at Westminster Abbey, the Queen created her son Duke of York, Earl of Inverness and Baron Killyleagh.

1977   *1987*   *1997*

103

The Golden Years

In 1986 the Queen and Prince Philip reached milestone birthdays. There were national celebrations for hers on 21st April with a service of Thanksgiving at St. George's Chapel, Windsor, before a balcony appearance and the receiving of flowers from hundreds of schoolchildren in the forecourt of Buckingham Palace, and a walkabout in Covent Garden before a gala show 'Fanfare for Elizabeth' at the Royal Opera House. All day, television channels were devoted to the Queen's 'sixty glorious years'. By contrast, strictly private celebrations were held for Prince Philip's 65th birthday on 10th June.

Quiet Prince Philip's birthday may have been, but by October 1986 he was firmly in the public eye. During their historic visit to China, the first ever of a British monarch, the Duke told a British student in the crowd, 'If you stay here much longer you will go back with slitty eyes.' The Press Secretary was quick to point out that no insult had been intended. 'Jocular comments have been taken totally out of context,' he insisted.

1947   *1957*   *1967*

Dawn of a Dynasty

FAR LEFT: *The Queen is presented with flowers as she is driven through Covent Garden for a 60th birthday tribute in her honour at the Royal Opera House, April 1986*

LEFT: *The Queen autographs a book while visiting a family in China as part of the Hong Kong tour, October 1986*

BELOW: *The Queen on the visit to China, October 1986*

    The Queen never gives autographs, but when on a visit to Hong Kong eight-year-old Raymond Tung shyly asked for her signature, she laughingly obliged. As if to prove that they were fit, even though both of an age when the average person retires, the Queen and the Duke walked further along the Great Wall of China than had been planned, as if to prove a point. They visited the Forbidden City in Peking and, like any tourist, gazed in wonder at some of the recently excavated 6,000 life-size terracotta warriors that guard the tomb of Emperor Qin Shi Huang. It was an unusual inspection of the Guard.

    When their visit came to an end - only the second State Visit to a Communist country - the Queen and Prince Philip were given a spectacular send-off by 2,000 colourfully costumed Chinese dancers. Unfortunately they returned home to a personal family crisis.

1977   *1987*   *1997*

The Golden Years

Their youngest son, Prince Edward, had become increasingly unhappy in the Royal Marines and eventually, in January 1987, announced his decision to leave. A brave and difficult decision for him, which won him much sympathy from the British public. In a leaked letter to Prince Edward's commandant-general, Prince Philip revealed his 'sadness' at his son's decision. The Queen and the Duke continued to support Prince Edward in his choice of career, feeling slight guilt that their children had suffered through having such high profile parents.

In her Birthday Honours List that year the Queen gave their only daughter the title 'Princess Royal' in honour of her tireless charity work. A universally popular decision. As a concession to age, the Queen decided not to ride her horse Burmese in the 1987 Trooping the Colour, but used Queen Victoria's open landau instead.

LEFT: *The Queen at the Trooping the Colour, June 1986*

RIGHT: *The Queen and Diana ride at Sandringham, January 1987*

1947   *1957*   *1967*

Dawn of a Dynasty

Troubled with arthritis, Prince Philip gave up the more dangerous four-in-hand carriage driving in favour of the less strenuous two-in-hand, which he still does today - taking part in the Stanmer Horse Trials near Brighton in May 1997. Prince Philip has long suffered with a painful right hand, said to have been caused originally by over-enthusiastic handshaking. The Queen and the Duke of Edinburgh's record came at a reception in Washington where they shook 1,547 hands in one hour.

In November 1987 they celebrated their Ruby Wedding Anniversary. As so often in the past, they spent the anniversary in the calm of Luton Hoo, a stately home in Bedfordshire (where the Queen's grandmother became engaged at a ball in 1891). This day was sacred to them and they chose to spend it alone, away from the family and the public gaze.
On such a day, titles and position are irrelevant and they become simply Elizabeth and Philip. Husband and wife.

1977   1987   1997

1947   1957   1967

THE
Overriding the Storms
87-97
ROYAL DECADE

1977   1987   1997

The Golden Years

1987 - 1997
Overriding the Storms

After forty years of marriage and a thirty-five year reign, it would have been forgivable to suppose that the path ahead would be smooth for the Queen and Prince Philip. With three of their children married, sufficient heirs to continue the line of succession well into the next century, decades of experience fulfilling some hundred thousand official engagements throughout the world, and an unparalleled international popularity, their lives appeared to be reliably secure.

But as the next decade unfolded they faced some of the greatest challenges they had ever known.

Since the screening of the *Royal Family* documentary in 1969, the distinction between their public and private lives had begun to blur. With media interest in 'Diana and Fergie' at its height, so the appetite for personal information increased. In the autumn of 1987 the Queen and Prince Philip were photographed with all their grandchildren for the first time. The relaxed portrait, taken at Balmoral by Karsh of Ottawa, was used by the Queen and the Prince on their Christmas cards that year until they discovered that the private photograph had been pirated by a tabloid newspaper. It was an unexpected intrusion.

PREVIOUS PAGE: *The Queen at Dunblane primary school, March 1996*

BELOW: *The Queen being photographed at Windsor Horse Show, May 1988*

1947   1957   1967

Overriding the Storms

MILESTONES
87-97

1987
The Queen and Duke of Edinburgh celebrated their Ruby Wedding Anniversary

1991
The Queen spoke to the nation on television in first ever war broadcast

1992
State apartments at Windsor Castle badly damaged by fire

1994
The Queen, Duke of Edinburgh and Royal Family attended a Service of Thanksgiving and Remembrance to mark 50th anniversary of D-Day held in Portsmouth. Followed by review of Allied Fleet in the Solent and flypast of World War II aircraft

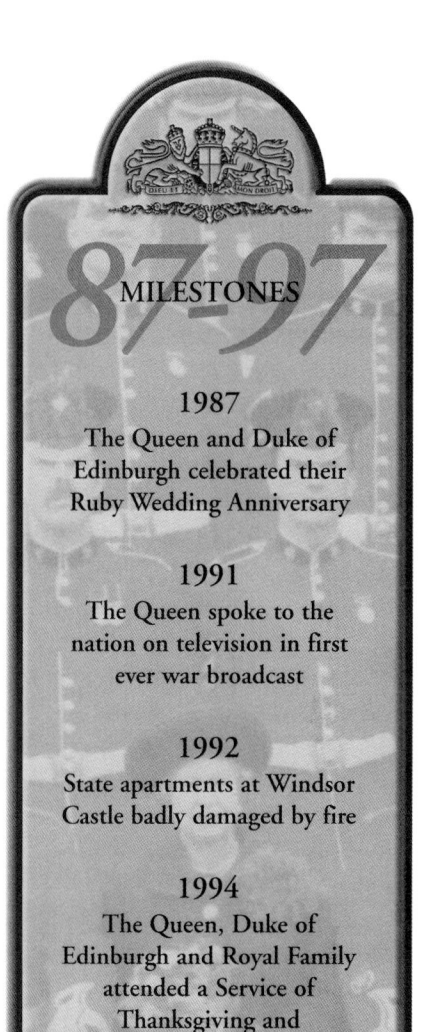

1996
70th birthday of Queen Elizabeth II

1977 *1987* *1997*

The Golden Years

ABOVE: *The Queen smiles in the rain at a polo match in Windsor Great Park, July, 1988*

RIGHT: *The Royals pose for photographs after a service at Sandringham Church. L to R: Duchess of York, Queen Mother, Duke of York, Princess of Wales, Prince Charles, Peter Phillips, Prince William, Zara Phillips, Duke of Edinburgh, Princess Margaret and the Queen. December 1988*

In March 1988 the Prince of Wales was involved in a tragedy whilst skiing at Klosters, when one of his friends Major Hugh Lindsay was killed in an avalanche. Major Lindsay had been appointed equerry to the Queen in 1983 and his wife worked in the Palace press office. The Royal Family found that private grief became very public news. Instead of withdrawing behind palace walls and becoming more remote, the Queen and Prince Philip realised that the world was changing and they had got to swim with the tide or sink.

As if to prove that they were in touch with modern issues, the Duke of Edinburgh became Patron of the European Year of the Environment and publicly attacked the 'arrogance' of the human race in claiming to have 'conquered nature'. Addressing the Royal Society of Arts he warned that one-third of all life forms could be extinct within 60 years, with up to 10,000 species a year being destroyed. It was a speech that shocked. During a State Visit of King Olav of Norway in April 1988 the Queen voiced her own concerns about pollution in the North Sea. That year all the Royal Family's cars were converted to use lead-free petrol.

A week later the Queen and Prince Philip were in Australia for the country's bi-centennial celebrations. There they were presented with a new 'high-tech' State Coach, funded by public donations. The aluminium carriage with electronic windows is now used each year for the State Opening of Parliament. The vehicle had not cost the British taxpayer a penny. In Australia the royal couple appeared to be more relaxed than usual, their popularity undiminished. At a garden party for the Queen's birthday a ballot had to be held when 10,000 people applied for the 1,200 tickets. On a visit to the outback it was revealed that the Aborigines call the Queen 'Yoga Bidyer', translated as 'Boss Lady'. Prince Philip roared with laughter.

1947 *1957* *1967*

Overriding the Storms

After Australia's bi-centenary, in July 1988 the Queen and Prince Philip visited the Netherlands for the tercentenary of the Glorious Revolution, which had brought William of Orange to the British throne. Although the present Queen Beatrix came to the Dutch throne on her mother Juliana's abdication, Queen Elizabeth II was adamant that she would not be stepping down herself. Later in the year she and Prince Philip visited Torbay in Devon to mark the 300th anniversary of William of Orange's arrival in Britain. They were joined by Queen Beatrix's son William, the present Prince of Orange. As with so many royal engagements, history and the twentieth century moved in tandem.

At 8.18am on 8th August 1988 the Queen and Prince Philip became grandparents once again, when the Duchess of York gave birth to her first child - Princess Beatrice. The Duchess received much criticism for going to Australia ten days later, leaving her baby behind. The censure marked a decline in her popularity. A second daughter, Princess Eugenie, was born on 23rd March 1990.

As an extensive re-wiring and renovation programme began at Windsor Castle, which would take many years to complete, the Royal Family spent Christmas at Sandringham for the first time since 1965. For the Queen and Prince Philip it was a reminder of more carefree days. As New Year 1989 dawned, a nationwide Gallup Poll revealed that 80% of the British public preferred having a monarch to an elected Head of State. Three-quarters of those questioned wanted the Queen to have more influence over Affairs of State, and 86% felt that the Royal Family should speak out on environmental issues. The results were heart warming for the Queen and the Duke.

1977   *1987*   *1997*

The Golden Years

In April 1989 the Queen formally accepted an invitation from President Gorbachev to visit Russia. An historic decision that would have seemed impossible even a decade earlier. The Princess Royal made a 17 day tour of Russia in May 1990, testing the water for her parents, but the Soviet political climate was such that four more years were to pass before the Queen and Prince Philip could actually make the journey themselves.

In the spring of 1989 they made a less controversial visit to Barbados to celebrate the 350th anniversary of the island's parliament. As a sign of the times, it was a short flying visit despite the distance. Likewise, on 1st June American President George Bush made a *one* day trip to Britain, lunching with the Queen at Buckingham Palace. The days when an official Commonwealth visit lasted several months had gone forever.

A welcome return to a more leisurely way of life came briefly for the Queen and Prince Philip on an official visit to the Channel Islands. Over three relaxed days they travelled in horse-drawn carriages and small open boats, and the islanders witnessed many informal moments. When a nervous child dropped a single rose, the Queen quickly retrieved it from the ground before the flower was trampled underfoot. Behind the Queen and the Duke's smiles, however, lay a personal sorrow. The marriage of their only daughter had collapsed and within weeks news of the formal separation would be made public.

LEFT: *The Queen visits the Channel Islands, May 1989*

TOP RIGHT: *The Queen, Queen Mother and Prince and Princess of Wales enjoy the tug of war at the Braemar Games, September 1989*

RIGHT: *The Queen and Prince Philip in transit on their visit to the Channel Islands, May 1989*

1947   *1957*   *1967*

Overriding the Storms

As the years passed and the reign lengthened, the Queen and Prince Philip inevitably began to make return visits to various countries. Nowhere did they witness greater changes than on a four day visit to Singapore in October 1989. The official programme was deliberately designed to show how the republic had altered since their previous visit seventeen years earlier. A cruise down the river gave an excellent panoramic view of the transformed landscape with its many skyscrapers; they toured a new town with a population of 250,000, visited the parliament building and a university, and lunched with the Prime Minister on the 74th floor of Singapore's tallest building. There could have been no greater contrast to their tour of the Channel Islands.

1977   *1987*   *1997*

115

The Golden Years

From Singapore they travelled on to Malaysia for the Commonwealth Heads of Government meeting. They opened the new British High Commission in Kuala Lumpur and had an encounter with an Oriental 'dragon'. Typically, Prince Philip looked under the colourful red and gold costume to see who was inside. While visiting the national Mosque of Alam Shah, the Queen had to wear a long kimono style robe and slippers to comply with local custom. With evidence of the minutiae that is included in the planning of royal tours, the Queen had worn a bronze-coloured outfit that day which perfectly matched the colour of the robe. On almost every visit she will wear a piece of jewellery that is of some significance to the place, although only the most observant and knowledgeable appreciate the gesture.

On returning to Britain the Queen opened Parliament in November. It marked the beginning of an eight month experiment period of live television coverage of the House of Commons. Usually cameras were allowed into the Commons only for the Queen's speech; now viewers could see for the first time Her Majesty's government and the House of Lords in debate. As Head of State and closely involved with the country's politics, the Queen was anxious that the workings of Parliament should not remain a mystery to the public.

In February 1990 a visit to New Zealand became a family affair. Prince Edward opened the Commonwealth Games in Auckland and was later joined by his parents, who officially closed what many considered to be the most successful games ever. The Queen and Prince Philip then began their longest tour of the country since 1953.

With often 30 different events on their schedule each day, a number of engagements were deliberately tailored to suit the Queen and Prince Philip's personal interests. While the Prince, as a keen yachtsman, started the third leg of the Whitbread Round the World Yacht Race, the Queen opened the Auckland Racing Club's new grandstand at Ellerslie for the Queen Elizabeth II Stakes. The main reason for the tour, however, was the Waitangi Day celebrations to mark the 150th anniversary of the Treaty in which Maoris ceded governorship of the colony to Great Britain in return for guaranteed possession of their land.

1947 *1957* *1967*

Overriding the Storms

Many Maoris believe that the Treaty was not honoured and, not for the first time, the Queen faced protests. This time, before a crowd of 30,000, she silenced demonstrators and received rapturous applause when she unexpectedly made part of her speech in Maori, acknowledging that there had been weaknesses in the Treaty and stressing a 'legacy of promise' that matters would improve.

In Australia the Queen and Prince Philip appear to enjoy the lack of formality that they encounter, which seems to rub off on them. During a lunch at the Commonwealth Games, the Queen noticed that New Zealand swimmer Paul Kingsman had not received a salad and so passed her own on to him. Back in England the couple were noticeably more approachable. When they visited London Zoo in the summer of 1990 to open the new Lifewatch Centre, once the formalities were over, they became tourists for a day and almost received a soaking from a mischievous bathing elephant as they wandered around.

LEFT: *Prince Philip, the Queen, Queen Mother and the Prince and Princess of Wales meet pipers at the Braemar Games, September 1989*

ABOVE: *The Queen Mother, the Queen and the Duke of Edinburgh share a joke at Epsom, June 1990*

1977   1987   1997

The Golden Years

That summer Prince Philip became the first member of the Royal Family to take part in a radio advertisement. Joining forces with actors Warren Mitchell and Dennis Waterman, he appealed for funds for the British Sports Trust. It was a new approach to charity work. At the Queen's Gallery at Buckingham Palace an unusual exhibition of royal memorabilia went on display for the first time, including the Queen's own handwritten account of her parent's Coronation when she was eleven years old.

While the pattern of official engagements stays predictably the same, each individual event will have a highlight that the Queen and Prince Philip remember. This can be a moment of humour, an unusual angle, or a rare occasion when plans go awry. Every year there are two visits to Britain by a foreign Head of State. Each is treated with full ceremony, stays at Windsor or Buckingham Palace with their entourage, and the itinerary follows a very set pattern.

LEFT: *Prince Philip and King Constantine of Greece on Yeoman, during Cowes week, August 1990*

RIGHT: *The Queen opens the Devizes lock flight on the Kennet and Avon Canal, August 1990*

1947   1957   1967

Overriding the Storms

It would seem likely that these visits all blend in to one, and yet strangely each stands out. When President Ceausescu of Romania visited he was the first leader of a Communist country to stay at Buckingham Palace. The Queen and Prince Philip were warned in advance by the French President that Ceausescu would steal anything that was not screwed down and kept a vigilant watch on him.

In the spring of 1990 the Queen and Prince Philip were about to leave the Palace to meet President Venkataraman of India when a security scare forced them to remain inside and arrangements had to be changed at the last minute. That October, President Cossiga of Italy arrived with a gift of 100 Tuscan oak trees. One of the most extraordinary State Visits that the Queen and Prince Philip must have encountered was that of Lech Walesa, President of Poland, who stayed at Windsor Castle in April 1991. Ten years earlier he had been a shipyard electrician in Gdansk and leader of the banned union Solidarity. Now he was President and paying a four day visit to Britain. Walesa could only speak two words of English, 'and they were quite colourful words,' the Queen admitted.

Despite having travelled widely, there are still surprisingly countries that the Queen and Prince Philip have not visited. In June 1990 they went to Iceland for the first time before flying on to Canada. Only days earlier the Queen's favourite horse *Burmese* had died. Originally a gift from the Canadian Royal Mounted Police, the Queen had ridden *Burmese* at eighteen Trooping the Colours.

Although they had visited Canada many times, on this occasion there was a conflict between French Canadians and English-speaking Canadians. Again the Queen tried to be a figure of unity. 'It is my fondest wish for this Canada Day,' she said before a crowd of 70,000, 'that Canadians come together and remain together, rather than dwelling on the differences which might further divide them.'

1977   1987   1997

The Golden Years

LEFT: *The Queen flanked by the Prince of Wales and the Duke of Edinburgh leaving Buckingham Palace for the Trooping the Colour, June 1991*

RIGHT: *The Queen and Prince Philip at the welcoming home of heroes and heroines of the Gulf War, June 1991*

There was no disunity in the United Kingdom, however, when the nation celebrated the Queen Mother's 90th birthday on 4th August. Earlier the Queen Mother visited the East End of London, as she had done during the blitz to lift spirits. Sprightly as ever, she made an unscheduled stop at the Blacksmith's Arms for a glass of Fuller's Bitter. In 1990 the Duke of York was thirty, the Princess Royal forty, and Princess Margaret was sixty. The Queen and Prince Philip hosted a party for them all in December to celebrate.

While the mother of the Queen was universally saluted, Prince Philip's mother was quietly laid to rest in a cemetery on the Mount of Olives in Jerusalem. Because of political unrest, her body had remained at Windsor for 19 years until arrangements could be made in accordance with her wishes. With continued political complications it was considered unsafe for Prince Philip to attend the ceremony.

In the year of the Queen Mother's nostalgic return to the East End, the 50th anniversary of the Battle of Britain was commemorated across the country. As the Queen and the Duke of Edinburgh stood on the balcony of Buckingham Palace to watch a flypast of 160 military aircraft and attended various anniversary events that summer, thoughts of an imminent war were very much in mind.

1947 *1957* *1967*

Overriding the Storms

Saddam Hussein's invasion of Kuwait in August 1990 precipitating the Gulf War of 1991, brought memories of the Falklands Conflict back to the Queen and Prince Philip. In her Christmas message the Queen sombrely expressed her hopes that servicemen out in the Gulf would soon be reunited with their families.

As the crisis escalated into battle, in January and February 1991 the Queen and the Royal Family made a series of morale-boosting visits to offer support and comfort. The Queen went to RAF Laarbruch in Germany, where she met crews of tornado squadrons preparing to leave for the Gulf. With Prince Philip, she went to Portsmouth Royal Naval Dockyard, speaking particularly to wives and families left behind. On 24th February the Queen made a televised speech to the nation in which she expressed hope for a just and lasting peace. The war ended four days later. A victory parade was held in London on 21st June, with the Queen taking the salute from the Mansion House.

1977   1987   1997

The Golden Years

A State Visit to America was used by the Queen as an opportunity to offer her thanks to the Americans for their part in the Gulf War, and to award an honorary knighthood to the leader of Desert Storm, General Norman Schwarzkopf. On arrival in Washington the Queen spoke outside the White House and found herself hidden behind a bank of microphones. Millions of television viewers saw only her hat. When she spoke at a joint meeting of Congress two days later, she quipped 'I do hope you can all see me today?'

On 10th June 1991 Prince Philip celebrated his 70th birthday and reluctantly agreed to a more public party than he would have wished, held in the grounds of Windsor Castle. Some 6,000 people bought tickets for the party and a banquet was arranged for a further 1,500. Inspired by the Duke of Edinburgh's Award Scheme, there were gold, silver and bronze tables for the entertainment at differing prices. The event raised £1 million for various charities.

With no sign of slowing down, after returning from America with the Queen, the Duke of Edinburgh immediately flew off to Sweden for a World Wildlife Fund meeting. In 1990 he had conducted 554 official engagements, not counting many private meetings in the line of duty that go unrecorded.

1947   *1957*   *1967*

Overriding the Storms

On 7th October the Queen and Prince Philip flew to Namibia, the newest member of the Commonwealth, and then to drought-stricken Zimbabwe. 'I pray that the drought may end soon,' said the Queen in a speech, 'and that you will have ample rain in the coming year.' At that precise moment the heavens opened and torrential rain swept the region. 'Stay long, stay long, stay!' came the cry from thousands of people lining the route to Bulawayo airport. But duty called.

In her 1991 Christmas Day message the Queen gave a clear indication that she will never abdicate. 'Over the years I have tried to follow my father's example and to serve you as best I can. I feel the same obligation to you now that I felt in 1952,' she said, and vowed to continue with 'your prayers, and your help and with the love and support of my family, I shall try to serve you in the years to come.'

When the Queen and Prince Philip went to Church the following Sunday at Sandringham, the usual crowd of well-wishers had swelled to 6,000, applauding her declaration. With rumours concerning the breakdown of the Prince and Princess of Wales' marriage, the Queen aimed to show the stability of the monarchy.

FAR LEFT: *The Queen and Duke of Edinburgh attend a 41 gun salute in Hyde Park to celebrate the Duke's 70th birthday, June 1991*

LEFT: *The Queen and Duke of Edinburgh meet President Gorbachev and his wife Raisa, July 1991*

ABOVE: *The Duke on his 70th birthday in Hyde Park*

The Golden Years

On 6th February 1992 the Queen had been on the throne for forty years a Ruby Jubilee, although with a far-reaching economic recession the Queen demanded that there be no public money spent on celebration. To mark the occasion, for the first time since the *Royal Family* documentary of 1969, the Queen allowed cameras to follow her for a whole year. The resulting film - *Elizabeth R* was a fly-on-the-wall documentary about her life and work. Besides royal duties and official ceremonies, there were many private moments seen for the first time. The Queen putting on the Imperial State Crown before opening Parliament; winning a sweepstake at the Derby; with her grandchildren at Sandringham; dancing at the gillies' ball at Balmoral, and dealing with her correspondence. In a telling moment she explained that younger members of her family find the regimented side of Royal life difficult, knowing what you will be doing a year in advance. 'It is a question of maturing into something ... and accepting the fact that here you are - and it is your fate. It is a job for life.'

LEFT: *The Queen out riding in Windsor Great Park on her 66th birthday, April 1992*

TOP RIGHT: *The Duke of Edinburgh at the Royal Windsor Horse Show, April 1993*

RIGHT: *The Queen and Duke of Edinburgh at the State Opening of Parliament, May 1992*

1947   *1957*   *1967*

Overriding the Storms

The programme was well received, but as it focused very much on the Queen's life, Prince Philip remained deliberately in the background. The anniversary itself was spent at Sandringham. First a simple Church service at which the Queen took Holy Communion, then it was a normal working day that included a visit to Tapping House in Snettisham, a day-care hospice for cancer patients. More publicly, the Queen and Prince Philip attended a performance of *Don Giovanni* at the Royal Opera House, Covent Garden, with their family. The Victoria and Albert Museum mounted the 'Sovereign' exhibition, for which the Queen loaned the breathtaking Coronation dress for display.

1977   *1987*   *1997*

The Golden Years

On 17th February 1992 the Queen and the Duke of Edinburgh flew out to Australia, only to find themselves making the headlines for unexpected reasons. A meeting between the Queen of Australia and a republican Prime Minister was bound to be newsworthy, but when Paul Keating placed an arm around the monarch's waist to guide her, royalists reeled in horror at his audacity. Touching the Queen was considered an insult, which was further exacerbated by his anti-British outburst in Parliament during the visit. Only the Queen appeared unperturbed. The patriotic Press took up her cause, with headlines screaming 'Off with his head!' Outwardly the couple remained relaxed and above the brouhaha. 'Hi, I'm James,' said a six year-old when the Queen opened a school on the outskirts of Canberra. 'Hello, I'm Elizabeth,' replied his sovereign.

Inevitably Paul Keating stirred up a storm at the time, and while Prince Philip made an official visit to New Zealand the Queen returned to England to face darkening skies. On the sixth anniversary of their engagement, the Duke and Duchess of York announced that their marriage was over. The Queen and Prince Philip knew privately that the Prince and Princess of Wales' relationship was in serious trouble too, and on 23rd April the Princess Royal was granted an uncontested Decree Nisi to formally end her marriage to Captain Mark Phillips. Of their three married children, all would soon be divorced. It was up to the Queen and Prince Philip to keep the royal show on the road.

LEFT: *The Queen chats to the Duchess of York in public for the first time since her separation from Prince Andrew, May 1992*

RIGHT: *The Royals on the balcony of Buckingham Palace after the Trooping the Colour, June 1992*

1947   *1957*   *1967*

Overriding the Storms

If republicans in Australia had begun to question the monarchy, a threat came closer to home with talk of Britain's closer integration with Europe. A tie that many feared could erode sovereignty altogether. In May 1992 the Queen went to Strasbourg to address the European Parliament for the first time. In an historic speech she spoke of the need to 'preserve the rich diversity of European countries' and warned against 'drab uniformity'. The 13 minute speech won a 12 minute standing ovation, although no-one could decide whether it had been pro or anti-European. There were, however, suggestions that she should become Queen of Europe.

Official visits to Malta, France, and Canada followed with record numbers of people turning out to see the Queen and Prince Philip.

If support for the monarchy was waning, there seemed little evidence to show it. In Ottawa a crowd of 100,000 awaited the Queen's arrival in a state landau and she had to delay making a speech until the overwhelming applause had died down.

1977 *1987* *1997*

The Golden Years

In October 1992 the Queen and Prince Philip made their first visit to Germany since re-unification, touring Dresden and in another historic moment walked through the Brandenburg Gate linking the East with the West. A man in the crowd pressed a piece of the demolished Berlin Wall into the Queen's hand, and she poignantly laid a wreath in tribute to the 192 East Germans who had been shot trying to cross the Wall. 'I believe I can say without indulging in petty rhetoric,' said German Foreign Minister Klaus Kinkel, 'that through this visit things have been put back in order.' Whether in the Commonwealth or in Europe, it seemed that the Queen still had an important role to play.

Having to attend a conference in Argentina meant that the Duke of Edinburgh had to be out of the country on their 45th wedding anniversary in November. The Queen intended to spend the day alone at Buckingham Palace, but a dramatic telephone call at midday meant a cancellation of all plans. Windsor Castle was on fire.

Shortly after 11.30am a hallogen spotlight caught a curtain alight in the private chapel. The fire quickly spread and raged all day and well into the night, gutting the historic St. George's Hall, scene of so many glittering State banquets. The Duke of York helped remove priceless works of art and told the Press that the Queen was 'utterly devastated' by the destruction. Windsor Castle has always been the one place that the Royal Family consider to be home. What should have been a year of joyous celebration turned out to be the worst of her reign.

ABOVE: *The Queen and Duke with Chancellor Kohl on the Royal visit to Germany, October 1992*

RIGHT: *The Queen's plea on the front page of The Daily Mail, November 1992*

1947   *1957*   *1967*

Overriding the Storms

Pictures of the Queen helplessly surveying the scene brought worldwide sympathy. At a Guildhall lunch intended to celebrate the 40th anniversary of her accession the Queen spoke emotionally, her voice still husky from smoke inhalation and shock. '1992 is not a year I shall look back on with undiluted pleasure,' she began. 'In the words of one of my more sympathetic correspondents, it has turned out to be an *annus horribilis.*' She accepted that the monarchy should be open to scrutiny, but appealed for 'gentleness, good humour and understanding.'

A few days later, Prime Minister John Major announced to the House of Commons that the Prince and Princess of Wales were to separate, bringing to an end months of intense speculation. Not just a marriage had ended, but the future of the heir to the throne now seemed uncertain.

RIGHT: *The Queen showing her grief while visiting Windsor Castle after the fire, November 1992*

1977   1987   1997

The Golden Years

The Queen and Prince Philip's year finished on a happier note when their daughter, the Princess Royal, married Commander Timothy Laurence on 12th December. Five years younger than his bride, Timothy James Hamilton Laurence was born in Camberwell, the son of a naval officer. In 1979 he had served on board the Royal Yacht *Britannia* and became an Equerry to the Queen in 1986. In contrast to her Westminster Abbey wedding in 1973, Princess Anne's second marriage was a small family affair at Crathie Parish Church near Balmoral.

To help pay for the restoration of Windsor Castle, the Queen and Prince Philip decided to open up the State rooms of Buckingham Palace to the general public for the first time. It was an unexpected but popular move. Within hours of coming on sale 40,000 advance group tickets were sold out for the first three years. A record number of tourists flocked to Windsor to see the damage for themselves, 140,000 in January 1993 alone. Buckingham Palace officially opened on 7th August and received visitors at the rate of 8,000 a day. The Palace had come to the rescue of the Castle.

In May 1993 the Queen and Prince Philip went to Hungary, the first time since Richard the Lionheart that a ruling British monarch had visited, and the crowds were the largest for any visiting Head of State.

'All the crowds you see are here because they want to welcome the Queen,' President Goncz told the press. Communist rule had ended three years earlier and thousands of Hungarians waved Union Jacks. 'They have not been told what to do and given correct flags as in the old days,' said the President. The Queen and Prince Philip undertook thirty official engagements in four days, ranging from a State banquet to visiting a hostel for the homeless. They were encouraged by the warmth of the reception and returned home looking refreshed.

LEFT: *The Queen and President Goncz on her visit to Hungary, May 1993*

TOP RIGHT: *Anxious moments as the Queen awaits the results of a photo-finish, Epsom, June 1993*

RIGHT: *The Queen celebrating her win at Derby Day, on the 40th anniversary of her Coronation, with Enharmonic and jockey Frankie Dettori*

1947   1957   1967

Overriding the Storms

On the 40th anniversary of Coronation Day the Queen went to the Derby at Epsom. Although she did not fulfil her ambition of winning the actual Derby, her horse *Enharmonic* ridden by Frankie Dettori came first in the previous race, the Diomed Stakes. The joy on Her Majesty's face ended the myth that the Queen does not show emotion in public. As she entered the paddock to view the horses, a man shouted: 'I love you! I love the monarchy! Keep it going!' before being ejected by security men. - The Queen gave him a beaming nod of approval.

1977   1987   1997

131

The Golden Years

What the 1990's had shown the world was that Royalty were human. Their emotions were the same as anyone elses's, no matter how hard they try to conceal them. As the divorce rate in Britain increased, inevitably it would effect the Royal Family. Prince Philip, more than any, has always been a realist. In Ottawa he had once shocked a press conference by saying of the monarchy: 'If at any stage people feel that it has no further part to play, then for goodness' sake let's end the thing on amicable terms without having a row about it.' On a visit to Cyprus in October 1993 it was the Queen's turn to shock by suggesting that she or her successor might not remain Head of the Commonwealth.

At the opposite end of the emotional spectrum, the Queen and Prince Philip visited the site of the Lockerbie air disaster in Scotland to pay their respects to the 270 victims who died and their grieving relatives. Just as they had done after the Aberfan disaster, and the Queen was to do again after the Dunblane tragedy in 1996, they represented the people of Britain in expressing their sorrow.

Grief of a more personal nature came in September 1993 when the oldest member of the Royal Household died. Margaret MacDonald, known as 'Bobo', was the Queen's childhood nanny and then her personal maid for 60 years. Said to be the most influential member of her staff, other than Prince Philip 'Bobo' knew the Queen better than anyone. At the funeral the Queen could not conceal her tears.

1947   *1957*   *1967*

132

Overriding the Storms

'I find that as the years pass by, my capacity for being surprised has lessened,' she told Commonwealth Heads of Government. 'Nowadays I have enough experience, not least in racing, to restrain me from laying any money down on how many countries will be in the Commonwealth in 40 years time, who they will be and where their meeting will be held. I will certainly not be betting on how many of you will have the Head of the Commonwealth as your Head of State. I suppose the only reasonably safe bet is that there will be three absentees: Prince Philip, *Britannia* and myself. But you never know…'

At the end of 1993 it was the Princess of Wales' turn to shock, with the announcement that she was withdrawing from public life and relinquishing most of her patronages - placing a greater workload on the remaining members of the Royal Family.

FAR LEFT: *Remembrance Day at the Cenotaph, November 1993*

ABOVE: *The Queen and Prince Philip at the State Opening of Parliament, November 1993*

LEFT: *Members of the Royal Family arrive for a carol service at the Church of St. Mary Magdalane. L to R: Prince Edward, Duke of Edinburgh, Prince Charles, Peter Phillips and Prince Andrew, December 1993*

The Golden Years

As Diana stepped out of the limelight, a new figure stepped in. Prince Edward's girlfriend, Sophie Rhys-Jones began to attract media attention to such an extent that Edward wrote to newspaper editors requesting privacy. There was fear that the Di-mania of 1981 would start all over again. With the marriages of his brothers and sister having failed, the Queen and Prince Philip insisted that their youngest son did not rush into an engagement. With the benefit of experience they offered Edward and Sophie every opportunity to be together, with no pressure to tie the knot.

LEFT: *Prince Philip and President Mugabe, President of the Republic of Zimbabwe on their way to the carriage that would take them to lunch at Buckingham Palace, May 1994*

RIGHT: *The Queen and Duke of Edinburgh unveil a memorial to Canada's war dead, June 1994*

1947   *1957*   *1967*

Overriding the Storms

While spending the New Year at Sandringham in 1994, the Queen fell from her horse fracturing her left wrist. When she and Prince Philip made an eight country tour of the Caribbean in February, her arm was incongruously in plaster. A number of coloured slings were made to match her outfits. During the tour the Royal Yacht clocked up one million miles of sea travel and the Queen performed a private ceremony in *Britannia's* engine room by cutting a red ribbon. Soon, however, would come the news that the ship would be scrapped, leaving Royal service in 1997. After taking the Royal Family to Scotland in August 1997, a valedictory cruise around the coastline of Britain was planned as *Britannia's* swan-song.

1977   *1987*   *1997*

The Golden Years

On returning from the Caribbean, the Queen and Prince Philip were surprised to discover that their marriage certificate along with a number of royal documents had been stolen from the Public Record Office and was being offered for sale on the black market. Police recovered the certificate in a Merseyside council house and three men were sentenced to 200 hours' community service.

With a piece of royal history safely restored, the Queen and Prince Philip came face to face with the most historic of all royal symbols - the Crown Jewels. The Queen officially opened a new £10 million Jewel House at the Tower of London, which was only the second time that she had actually seen the whole collection. Up to 20,000 people a day now see the spectacular jewels, which belong to the State and not the Queen personally. The Queen stood for a long time staring at St. Edward's Crown which she had last worn on Coronation Day.

1947   *1957*   *1967*

Overriding the Storms

On St. George's Day 1994 it was announced that the Princess Royal was to be bestowed with the title of Lady of the Most Noble Order of the Garter, a personal gift from the sovereign and given in recognition of Anne's outstanding achievements in charity work. The investiture took place at Windsor Castle on 13th June. With the Princess of Wales no longer in line to be Queen, Anne was a senior Royal figure who could be considered a consort for King Charles III at his Coronation. No decisions have been made, but the Queen had to keep all her options open to ensure the continuation of the monarchy. Just in case Prince Charles decided to step out of the line of succession, the Duke of York resigned from the Navy in readiness to act as Prince Regent in the event of the Queen's sudden death before Prince William reached eighteen.

As the Queen and Prince Philip undertook their usual punishing schedule of engagements, history continued to vie with the present. In May 1994 they travelled under the sea for the first time when the Queen opened the new Channel Tunnel, linking England and France. A month later they were taking part in events on both sides of the Channel for the 50th Anniversary of the D-Day Landings. In a spectacular climax 10,000 veterans marched past the Queen and the Duke on the Normandy beaches.

FAR LEFT: *The Queen at the D-Day celebrations at Southsea memorial, June 1994*

ABOVE: *The Royal Party at the Trooping the Colour, June 1994*

LEFT: *The Royals lead the family tribute at the Drumhead service, June 1994*

1977 *1987* *1997*

The Golden Years

After some five years of planning, the Queen and Prince Philip finally visited Russia in October 1994. At the start of the reign, the idea of the Queen walking into the Kremlin to greet a Russian leader would have been an impossible scenario. Now, in a vastly changed political climate, she became the first reigning British monarch to set foot on Russian soil. They met President Yeltsin at the Kremlin, undertook a walkabout in Red Square, and watched the Bolshoi Ballet. On a visit to St. Petersburg they saw the tombs of thirty six Tsars and their families, soon to be joined by the remains of Nicholas II. Prince Philip had given a blood sample to enable bones of the murdered Tsar to be identified. His relationship can be traced back on his mother's side of the family.

1947　　　　　　　　　　*1957*　　　　　　　　　　*1967*

Overriding the Storms

Ten days after the Russian tour, Prince Philip made a private visit to Israel to see his mother's grave for the first time. He also received a 'Righteous Gentile' award from the Holocaust Memorial Centre in his mother's honour for her work in saving Jews during World War II by hiding a family in her home.

Prince Philip recalled how he had seen anti-Semetic hostility himself in the 1930's. Having been transferred from a school in England to Salem, he had witnessed a Jewish boy being overpowered and having his hair cut off. The Prince lent the boy his cricket cap to wear until the hair grew back. 'It may have been trivial, but I have never forgotten this act of inhumanity,' he said. 'The Holocaust may be over, but there are altogether too many examples in the world today of man's capacity for inhumanity.' After planting a tree in memory of his mother, he wrote in the visitors' book, 'God brings everything we do to judgement.'

LEFT: *To the strains of Colonel Bogey, the Queen inspects a guard of honour at Moscow's Vnukovo II Airport, October 1994*

ABOVE: *The Queen and Prince Philip at St. Basil's Cathedral in Red Square, October 1994*

RIGHT: *Guests of the Queen and Prince Philip, Boris and Naina Yeltsin attend a photo-call before dining on Britannia in St. Petersburg, October 1994*

1977   1987   1997

The Golden Years

The changes in world politics that allowed the Queen to visit Russia and Prince Philip to go to Israel, also enabled them to fly to Northern Ireland during an IRA ceasefire in 1995. After opening a new bridge in Belfast they went on a walkabout in a much more relaxed atmosphere than on any previous visit, but were still guarded by armed RUC officers.

The end of apartheid in South Africa brought the country back into the Commonwealth after a thirty five year absence, providing a chance for the Queen and Prince Philip to visit. At ease in the company of President Mandela, they invited him to visit Britain in 1996. Travelling widely in Pretoria, Soweto and Durban over six days in March 1995, the Queen and Prince Philip were greeted by thousands of people, many of whom remembered her previous visit as Princess Elizabeth in 1947. Forty-eight years on, the Queen described her return to South Africa as 'one of the outstanding experiences of my life.'

LEFT: *The Queen, Prince Philip and Queen Noor of Jordan at the wedding of Crown Prince Pavlos of Greece at St. Sophias Cathedral, west London, July 1995*

1947 *1957* *1967*

Overriding the Storms

Throughout 1995 there were many events to commemorate the 50th anniversary of the end of World War II. The Queen and Prince Philip received addresses from both Houses of Parliament in Westminster Hall and attended a thanksgiving service in St. Paul's Cathedral to mark the Allied victory.

RIGHT: *The Queen and Duke of Edinburgh watching the racing at Epsom, June 1995*

BELOW: *The Queen and Nelson Mandela in a carriage procession along the Mall on the way to Buckingham Palace, July 1995*

1977   1987   1997

141

The Golden Years

That summer VE Day and VJ Day were celebrated anew and those too young to remember the war experienced the spirit of 1945. Crowds responded enthusiastically towards the Queen Mother, just as they had done fifty years before, and the focus was on the Royal Family throughout the rejoicing. In times of defeat people call down the government, Churchill had said; in times of victory they sing 'God Save the Queen'. A State dinner was held at the Guildhall attended by 50 political leaders; there was a marchpast of veterans along The Mall in front of the Queen (with Prince Philip marching as an ex-serviceman), and as the Royal Family gathered on the balcony of Buckingham Palace a lone Lancaster bomber let fall a cloud of red poppies in memory of those who had lost their lives fighting for King and country. At sunset on 8th May two minutes' silence was observed before the Queen lit a beacon in Hyde Park, setting off a chain of victory beacons across the country.

ABOVE: *An incredible sight, a Lancaster Bomber drops poppies over the crowds at Buckingham Palace, August 1995*

ABOVE RIGHT: *Royal Party during the VJ celebrations*

RIGHT: *The Queen at the Tower of London for the VJ service*

1947   *1957*   *1967*

Overriding the Storms

Even though the Royal Family faced many personal crises throughout the 1990's, thousands still thronged outside Buckingham Palace throughout the commemorations, in scenes that many had feared might never be witnessed again. In times of jubilation, it seemed, the nation not only wanted but expected the Queen and her family to be at the forefront. By the end of 1995, the Queen and Prince Philip had attended 1,272 official engagements that year and invitations continue to pour in daily.

On 20th November 1995 the Queen and Prince Philip celebrated 48 years of marriage and clocked up their own record. They had now beaten Edward VII's 47 years, to have the longest marriage of any monarch this century. Except for George III's 57 years, the Queen has been married longer than any other British sovereign.

The VE and VJ Day anniversary celebrations appeared to revive the bond between royalty and the people. The Commonwealth showed no sign of wanting to give up the Queen as its Head, and the only threat appeared to come from European union. Whether she will be the last Queen of England, only time will tell.

1977   1987   1997

The Golden Years

ABOVE: *Carrying a single daffodil, the Queen remembers the dead at Dunblane Cathedral, March 1996*

RIGHT: *The Queen at the Commonwealth Day service at Westminster, March 1996*

Arriving in New Zealand for the Commonwealth Heads of Government meeting at the end of 1995 the Queen signed her assent to an Act compensating a Maori tribe for lands confiscated by British colonists in 1863, healing a very old wound. In Australia, any ambitions Paul Keating had to achieve a Republic by the millennium ended in March 1996 when he was defeated in a General Election. Never complacent, however, the Queen and Prince Philip had begun holding twice yearly planning meetings with their family and advisors to discuss the way ahead. As a result, the Queen began paying income tax and made changes to the Civil List, conscious always of public opinion. 'It is worth pointing out,' said a Buckingham Palace spokesman, 'that one of the reasons the monarchy has lasted for over 1,000 years is that it is able to adapt and change as necessary, whilst retaining the overwhelming public support it enjoys.' A nationwide television debate in 1997 with a telephone poll came down in favour of the monarchy, confirming the Queen and Prince Philip's belief that the majority prefer a non-political Head of State.

In the year of the Queen's 70th and Prince Philip's 75th birthdays, they undertook more engagements than twenty years earlier, and their official programme continued to remain varied. The Queen became the first reigning monarch for more than 400 years to attend a Roman Catholic service when she went to Westminster Cathedral to mark the centenary of its foundation; she and Prince Philip paid State Visits to Poland, the Czech Republic and Thailand; and as with any year there were highlights and lowlights, sadness and joy. Few could forget the Queen's tears at Dunblane on Mother's Day when she visited the school where sixteen children and their teacher had been killed by gunman Thomas Hamilton four days before, or her smiles as she welcomed President Mandela to London in July 1996. The President was received with warmth by enthusiastic crowds, resulting in one of the most pleasurable State Visits that the Queen had experienced.

1947   *1957*   *1967*

Overriding the Storms

In 1997 the Queen and Prince Philip brought the monarchy a step closer to the twenty-first century when on 6th March a royal web site was launched on the Internet. More than a million accesses were made on the first day to read Royal profiles, history, speeches, and see pictures from the Queen's collection. Soon it was to become the world's most visited site, being accessed 6.25 million times a month. The web site of Britain's most successful pop group at the time, the Spice Girls, was visited just 2.5 million times per month. On 6th May 1997 the Queen's 165 pages were increased by a further 85, enabling computer users to 'tour' Buckingham Palace and receive news of royal visits.
'We have interest from all over the world,' said a Buckingham Palace spokesman, 'The Queen is very pleased.'

1977　　　*1987*　　　*1997*

The Golden Years

A Golden Wedding Anniversary offers any couple the opportunity to look back and a reason to celebrate the present. On 5th July 1997 the Queen and Prince Philip were due to attend a Royal Pageant of the Horse in Windsor Great Park, in which their joint love of equestrian events was to be used as the basis for a spectacular show to mark their special anniversary year. Over 1,000 horses were to take part in an extravaganza that would have included riding displays, colourful

Celebrating their fiftieth year of marriage in 1997, the Queen and Prince Philip have made the monarchy blossom without disturbing its roots. Their success has always been the link that they have forged between the present and the past. As a couple, they have symbolised stability even in the midst of chaos. As a working team, they have offered continuity over five decades.

After the Aberfan disaster of 1966 the Queen and Prince Philip travelled to Wales to show their compassion and offer comfort. On 9th May 1997 they returned to the scene and planted a tree in the Garden of Remembrance that has been made as a tribute, and met survivors. It was a sign that, even after thirty years, they had not forgotten. Despite the sad memories, a whole new generation of schoolchildren were there to greet them and it became a time to look forward with hope.

TOP: *The Queen is 70! At Sandringham Church, April 1996*

RIGHT: *The Queen with the Duke on his 75th birthday in Windsor, June 1996*

1947 *1957* *1967*

Overriding the Storms

ceremonies and musical performances, with a packed programme of events throughout the day. As it happened, the event had to be cancelled due to unseasonally heavy rain which turned the site into a quagmire.

On 15th July the Queen and Prince Philip hosted a Golden Wedding Garden Party at Buckingham Palace for 4,000 couples who had all been married in 1947. A day of reminiscence and pride, as a prelude to the more public celebrations planned for November.

Visiting the Royal Mint at Llantrisant in May 1997, the Queen and the Duke of Edinburgh struck the first Golden Wedding crown which commemorates their anniversary. Significantly it is also the first British coin of modern times that does not bear the Queen's head alone, but has a portrait of them both.

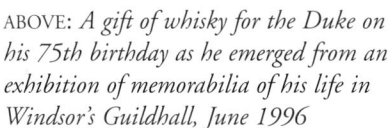

ABOVE: *A gift of whisky for the Duke on his 75th birthday as he emerged from an exhibition of memorabilia of his life in Windsor's Guildhall, June 1996*

LEFT: *The Queen and Nelson Mandela meet Phil Collins, July 1996*

1977   1987   1997

1947   *1957*   *1967*

A Golden Milestone

1977   1987   1997

The Golden Years

Although officially the reign of Queen Elizabeth the Second, unofficially it can be seen as no less than the reign of Elizabeth and Philip, for it has been a partnership. His behind-the-scenes influence has been as important as her higher profile contribution. Dovetailing together from a public point of view Elizabeth has never lost the essential mystique on which monarchy thrives; Philip has presented a very human face that has kept remoteness at bay, At times he has appeared too outspoken, but insists that 'you can't go on forever producing bromides and platitudes.'

Today Prince Philip remains as active and irascible as he was in 1947. He has never suffered fools gladly and has no time for sycophants. He retains a down-to-earth attitude in a position that could be so easily distanced from reality. It is the only way he knows how to survive.

Like any successfully married couple, the Queen and Prince Philip compliment each other by their differences. He enjoys progress and modernisation; she is steeped in tradition and is comfortable with Royal routine. Glancing in the back of her car you will find cassette tapes of military band music; she is still serenaded each morning by a lone bagpiper, not just because Queen Victoria was but because she actually enjoys it; when millions watched her in the 1992 documentary *Elizabeth R* absentmindedly playing with a paper-knife, without even realising it she used a knighting motion as if it were a ceremonial sword. She does not act at being monarch. Elizabeth is Queen with every fibre of her being.

Born into a world with fewer restrictions, Prince Philip has not always fitted easily in to royal routine and its unremitting pressures. Hence, he will undertake several overseas trips a year alone, when he can concentrate on the business in hand as a working man and not as a Prince of the Realm. Ultimately, however, he insists that he has one main function in life - to support and protect the Queen. In fifty years that has never changed.

On very rare occasions Prince Philip has been called upon to support the Queen in unexpected ways. On a visit to the Commonwealth Institute, Kensington, in May 1993 the Queen was due to make an address. As the chairman of the Governors invited her to speak, she was seen rummaging in her handbag. After an unexpected silence, the Queen stepped forward to the microphone. 'I am going to ask my husband to read my speech,' she said with a hint of embarrassment. Prince Philip's eyes twinkled as he explained, 'I'm afraid the Queen forgot to bring her glasses with her,' before delivering the seven page address on his wife's behalf. 'One appears to have made a spectacle of oneself,' were the next day's inevitable headlines.

LEFT: *Flashback to the Queen and Duke at the ceremony for their Silver Wedding anniversary. L to R: the Queen Mother, Prince Philip, the Queen November 1972*

1947   *1957*   *1967*

A Golden Milestone

On any public engagement together the Queen and Prince Philip have a self-evident rapport. There are little asides and invariably the hint of a private joke. Officially the Queen walks two paces in front of the Duke, but in private he becomes the stronger of the two. In front of friends they tease each other, there is good natured bickering, and the surprise that he will occasionally throw orders at her and she obeys. He is the only person in the world who feels able to talk to the Queen on an equal level, as a husband to a wife, and after fifty years together there is a mutual dependence.

When Prince Philip once expressed a wish for a front-door of their own that they could close behind them and be completely private, he received a door-key as a birthday present from his wife. It opens the door to the private and appropriately named Queen's Tower at Windsor. In return, the Prince had Wood Farm on the Sandringham estate renovated and gave his wife the key as a gift. In the 1970's particularly they would spend several weekends alone there, looked after only by a an estate worker's wife. It has become like a timeshare cottage for the Royal Family.

ABOVE: *The Queen ready to deliver an important speech at the Commonwealth Institute in Kensington explaining that she has forgotten her spectacles, May 1993*

BELOW: *The Duke of Edinburgh reads the Queen's prepared speech*

1977 *1987* *1997*

The Golden Years

At Balmoral the Queen and Prince Philip have a small log cabin as a retreat. With glittering palaces and castles at their disposal they relish being alone in simple surroundings and the feeling of freedom that these sanctuaries provide. When the position of the log cabin became widely known, Territorial Army Volunteers moved it to a secret location in time for their Balmoral holiday in 1987. Their annual summer break in Scotland is still the highlight of the year. When, for example, the Queen landed at Heathrow after a ten day visit to Canada in 1994, waiting to greet her were five corgis - Kelpie, Pharos, Phoenix, Flora and Swift - with Harris and Brandy, two dorgis (dachshund-corgi cross), who all boarded another plane with the Queen and flew immediately to Scotland.

In their fiftieth anniversary year the Queen and Prince Philip remain forward thinking in both their private and public lives. As 1997 dawned they were already planning a tour of Canada and their State Visit to India and Pakistan in October, half a century after both countries gained their independence from Britain. Of equal importance that month, the Commonwealth Heads of Government meeting in Edinburgh with a formal application from Fiji to rejoin the Commonwealth ten years after it became a republic, calling for the Queen to return as the island's constitutional monarch. On a personal level the Queen and Prince Philip have watched Windsor Castle rising from the ashes and look forward to the spring of 1998 when it will be fully restored to its former glory.

LEFT: *The Queen and Duke of Edinburgh arrive at Smith's Lawn, Windsor Great Park, June 1984*

MIDDLE: *Carving of the Queen and Prince Philip's initials entwined in a true lovers' knot at Liverpool Cathedral. Originally stencilled by them 30th March, 1949*

FAR RIGHT: *The Queen and Prince Philip at the Chelsea Flower Show, May 1997*

1947   *1957*   *1967*

A Golden Milestone

In March 1949 Princess Elizabeth and Prince Philip visited Liverpool when the great Cathedral, like their marriage was still in its infancy. Inside the Cathedral they stencilled their initials E and P - on to one of the stone pillars of the lower nave. The letters were later carved deep into the stone and entwined in a lovers' knot, to remain there for centuries to come. Like the carving, their relationship has mellowed with the years and has withstood the test of time. After fifty years together, the Queen and Prince Philip are living proof that royal marriages, like fairytales, can have a happy ending.

1977 *1987* *1997*

The Golden Years

The Monarchy from the Birth of Queen Victoria

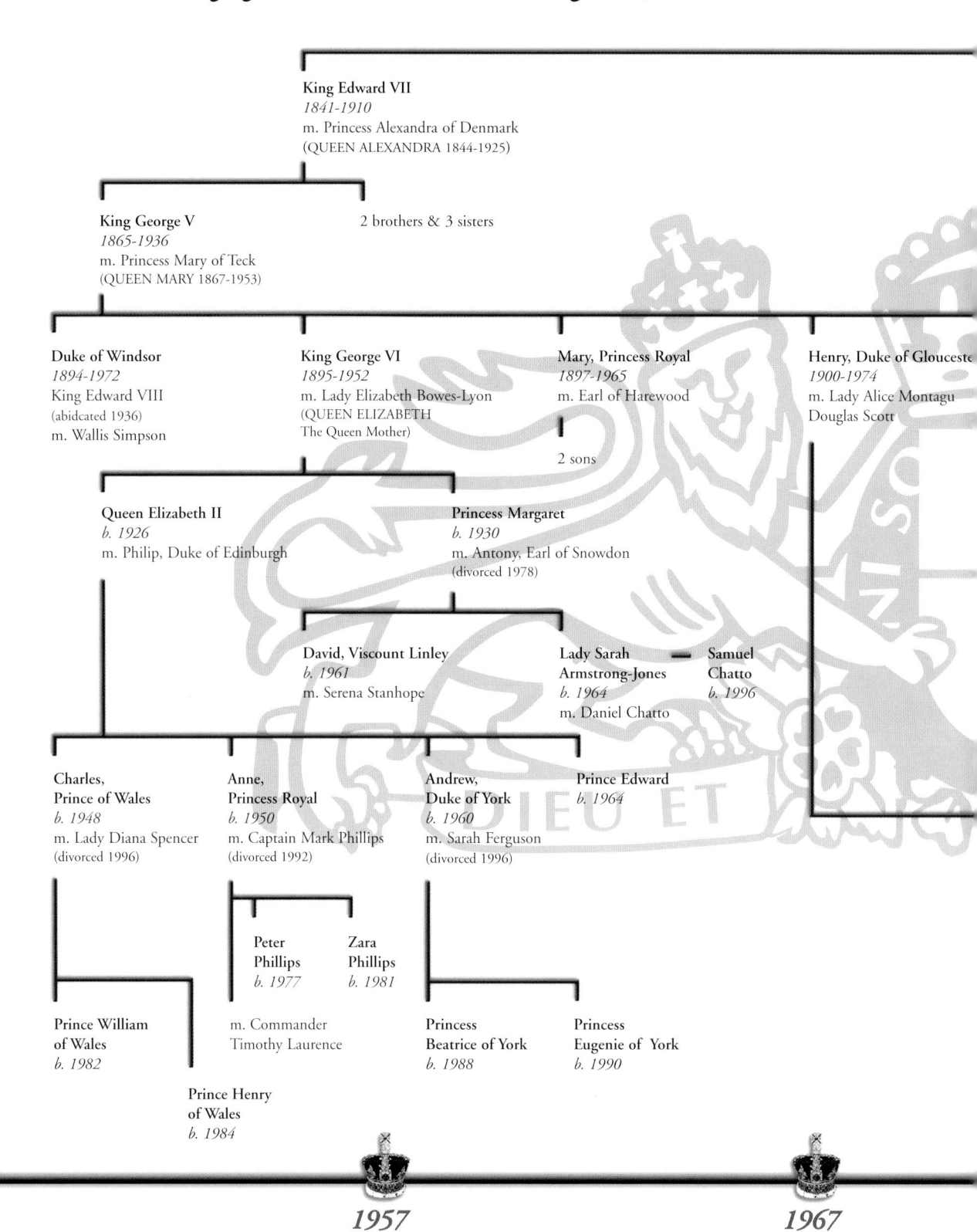

King Edward VII
1841-1910
m. Princess Alexandra of Denmark
(QUEEN ALEXANDRA 1844-1925)

King George V
1865-1936
m. Princess Mary of Teck
(QUEEN MARY 1867-1953)

2 brothers & 3 sisters

Duke of Windsor
1894-1972
King Edward VIII
(abidcated 1936)
m. Wallis Simpson

King George VI
1895-1952
m. Lady Elizabeth Bowes-Lyon
(QUEEN ELIZABETH
The Queen Mother)

Mary, Princess Royal
1897-1965
m. Earl of Harewood

2 sons

Henry, Duke of Glouceste
1900-1974
m. Lady Alice Montagu
Douglas Scott

Queen Elizabeth II
b. 1926
m. Philip, Duke of Edinburgh

Princess Margaret
b. 1930
m. Antony, Earl of Snowdon
(divorced 1978)

David, Viscount Linley
b. 1961
m. Serena Stanhope

**Lady Sarah
Armstrong-Jones**
b. 1964
m. Daniel Chatto

**Samuel
Chatto**
b. 1996

**Charles,
Prince of Wales**
b. 1948
m. Lady Diana Spencer
(divorced 1996)

**Anne,
Princess Royal**
b. 1950
m. Captain Mark Phillips
(divorced 1992)

**Andrew,
Duke of York**
b. 1960
m. Sarah Ferguson
(divorced 1996)

Prince Edward
b. 1964

**Peter
Phillips**
b. 1977

**Zara
Phillips**
b. 1981

**Prince William
of Wales**
b. 1982

m. Commander
Timothy Laurence

**Princess
Beatrice of York**
b. 1988

**Princess
Eugenie of York**
b. 1990

**Prince Henry
of Wales**
b. 1984

1947   *1957*   *1967*

The Family Tree

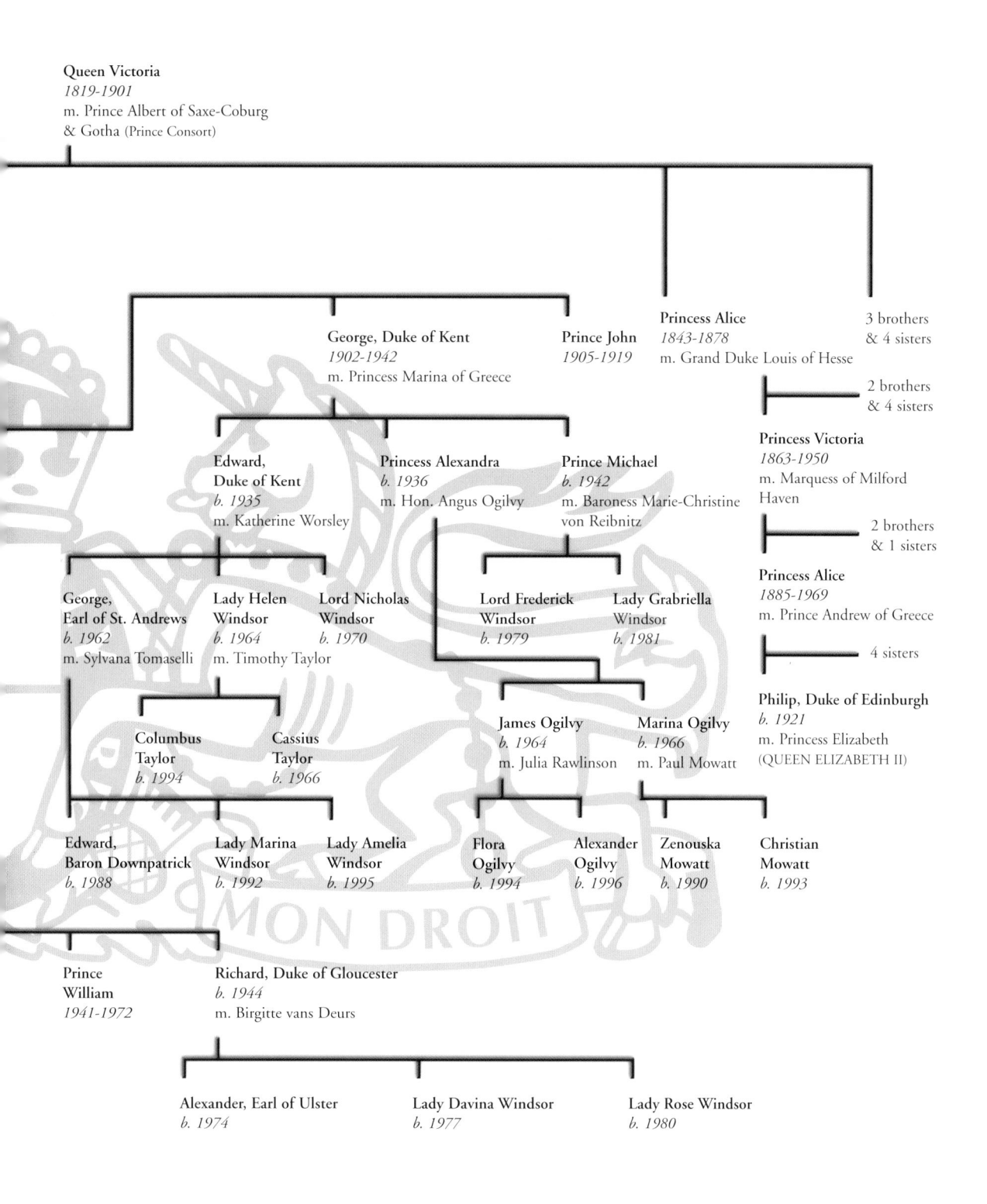

Queen Victoria
1819-1901
m. Prince Albert of Saxe-Coburg & Gotha (Prince Consort)

George, Duke of Kent
1902-1942
m. Princess Marina of Greece

Prince John
1905-1919

Princess Alice
1843-1878
m. Grand Duke Louis of Hesse

3 brothers & 4 sisters

2 brothers & 4 sisters

Edward, Duke of Kent
b. 1935
m. Katherine Worsley

Princess Alexandra
b. 1936
m. Hon. Angus Ogilvy

Prince Michael
b. 1942
m. Baroness Marie-Christine von Reibnitz

Princess Victoria
1863-1950
m. Marquess of Milford Haven

2 brothers & 1 sisters

Princess Alice
1885-1969
m. Prince Andrew of Greece

George, Earl of St. Andrews
b. 1962
m. Sylvana Tomaselli

Lady Helen Windsor
b. 1964
m. Timothy Taylor

Lord Nicholas Windsor
b. 1970

Lord Frederick Windsor
b. 1979

Lady Grabriella Windsor
b. 1981

4 sisters

Philip, Duke of Edinburgh
b. 1921
m. Princess Elizabeth (QUEEN ELIZABETH II)

Columbus Taylor
b. 1994

Cassius Taylor
b. 1966

James Ogilvy
b. 1964
m. Julia Rawlinson

Marina Ogilvy
b. 1966
m. Paul Mowatt

Edward, Baron Downpatrick
b. 1988

Lady Marina Windsor
b. 1992

Lady Amelia Windsor
b. 1995

Flora Ogilvy
b. 1994

Alexander Ogilvy
b. 1996

Zenouska Mowatt
b. 1990

Christian Mowatt
b. 1993

Prince William
1941-1972

Richard, Duke of Gloucester
b. 1944
m. Birgitte vans Deurs

Alexander, Earl of Ulster
b. 1974

Lady Davina Windsor
b. 1977

Lady Rose Windsor
b. 1980

1977   *1987*   *1997*

The Golden Years

RIGHT: *Trooping the Colour, the Mall, London, June 1997*

1947

1967

1977 *1987* *1997*

The Golden Years

THE GOLDEN YEARS
was produced by Solo Books Ltd
for the
DAILY MAIL *and* BRITISH PATHE *Plc*

THE BOOK
Representing Associated Newspapers
(publishers of the Daily Mail)
SIMON DYSON, ALLAN MARSHALL

Design
96HUNDRED DESIGN GROUP LTD

Design Team
PETER GATWARD, CHRISTINE MARTIN, SIMON RITCHIE AND GERALD GLOVER

Picture Researcher, Solo Books
DANNY HOWELL

Printing and Binding
INTEGRATED COLOUR EDITIONS EUROPE LTD
Book printed in Italy

THE VIDEO
Representing British Pathe Plc
CHRIS DAVIES, ROBERT JACKSON, MARTIN MORGAN

Project Creativity
PETER GATWARD

Project Publishing Director
DON SHORT, SOLO BOOKS LTD

DAILY MAIL	BRITISH PATHE	SOLO BOOKS LTD	96HUNDRED DESIGN GROUP LTD	INTEGRATED COLOUR EDITIONS EUROPE LTD
2 Derry Street,	60 Charlotte Street,	49-53 Kensington High Street,	182-194 Union Street,	Manor Close, Manor Road, Oving,
London W8 5TT	London W1P 2AX	London W8 5ED	London SE1 0LH	Aylesbury, Bucks HP22 4HW
	0171 323 0407	0171 376 2166	0171 401 9600	01296 640932

1947　　　*1957*　　　*1967*

The Golden Years

1977   1987   1997

DIEU ET MON DROIT